17 AMAZING MOMPRENEURS MAKING
MAGIC IN BUSINESS AND MOTHERHOOD

MOM MAGIC

mompreneur

*The magic of motherhood and how it's
changing the world.*

Angela Bell & Dr. Shellie Hipsky And 15 Inspiring Women Authors

ISBN: 979-8-9869367-3-4

Table of Contents

INTRODUCTION

The Inspired & Profitable Mompreneur was created by Angela Bell, to serve the need she saw and experienced as a mom; the need for time and financial freedom and flexibility. This need was all the more emphasized during the pandemic, when Moms around the world were overloaded by the ever-changing demands brought on by school & daycare closures, working from home, sick and fragile family members needing care, and communities needing love and support. She saw the need for moms to have the ability to continue making money, while simultaneously having flexible schedules, and work autonomy. Then, in 2021, she launched a podcast and online TV Show of the same name.

With the goal of showcasing, highlighting, and empowering Moms and Mompreneurs around the world, The Inspired & Profitable Mompreneur Podcast & TV Show serves as a platform for women to spread their message and knowledge, while also being a collection of resources for those who need them. It is now one of the most sought out Mom-based podcasts both nationally and internationally. You can find it on your favorite podcast platforms, such as Spotify, Google Podcasts, Apple Podcasts, iHeartRadio, and much more!

The Inspired & Profitable Mompreneur Community on Facebook, serves as a place where current and aspiring Mompreneurs can come together, share resources, support and encourage each other and seek guidance. Knowing that only moms can understand the unique needs and struggles of other moms, Angela is working to create an employer/job seeker site, to match up Moms looking to grow their team with mothers looking for flexible "mom-friendly" work.

Wanting to do more to elevate the status of Moms and Mompreneurs, Angela created the Mom Magic Anthology Series. This series will change the narrative around Moms in entrepreneurship, the work place, and life!

MOMS are the MAGIC in everything around us.

MOM Magic

The Magic of Motherhood and how it's changing the world!

This is for the moms who feel lost, exhausted, overwhelmed, and unacknowledged. For the moms who had dreams, and have put them on the back shelf. For the moms who know they have greatness inside of them, if they could only find a minute. We hear you! We see you! We are you! This book series was created for you, so you know you are not alone, you are a great mom, and there is a way!

The women in these books have struggled, lived and thrived in motherhood. They have made peace with the judgement and insane expectations of society, and they have found a way to live their best life! If they can do it, I promise you, SO CAN YOU! The stories, tools and methods shared in this book and the ones to follow, are a guide to help you live your best life too.

By you grabbing this book, it shows that you, too, are ready to show the world your **MOM MAGIC.**

The Inspired & Profitable Mompreneur offers:

- Inspired & Profitable Mompreneur Business Creation Packages
- Inspired & Profitable Mompreneur Public Relations
- Inspired & Profitable Mompreneur Podcast
- Inspired & Profitable Mompreneur Magazine (Launching Early 2023)
- Mompreneur Launch School
- Mompreneur Mastermind Group
- Inspired & Profitable Mompreneur Community

Moms are the key to creating a better, bright and more compassionate future for us all.

Mom Magic IS the Future...

With Love,
Angela Bell
The Inspired & Profitable Mompreneur

Angela Bell

Founder of The Inspired & Profitable Mompreneur

https://www.linkedin.com/in/angela-bell-776a529/
https://www.instagram.com/i.am.angelabell/
https://www.facebook.com/angela.bell.3597/
www.angelabell.ca

Angela is committed to helping moms create time & financial freedom through their own business. She is a multi-passionate entrepreneur, business & success coach for moms, and mom of twins. As the founder of the Inspired & Profitable Mompreneur, she uses her passion, training and experience to help other moms see themselves as the Queens they are and build their empire.

She has built a 7-figure food manufacturing business from the ground up, published 2 books - one of which was an international best seller, and helped hundreds of women launch and grow their own Inspired & Profitable online businesses.

Angela is committed to helping other moms live their very best lives, on their own terms!

In her spare time, you will find Angela playing with her kids and dogs, reading, baking, or going for a nice long-distance run.

YOU ARE THE MAGIC!

By Angela Bell

Mom Magic is the magical force that makes things happen and keeps life fun!

If you're a mom, then you know what mom magic is. You do it every day, even when you don't know you're doing it. To everyone else, though, it's an unknown force that keeps things together, keeps life fun, and gets stuff done. It's as important as water—maybe even more important. It is the foundation upon which everything else rests.

Do you remember when you were a kid and it seemed like your mom really could do magic? I sure do. I remember being a kid and thinking everything just magically fell into place. I remember being happy, feeling safe and loved, having great original Halloween costumes, and baking delicious cookies. I remember that the tooth fairy always came, the easter bunny had great hiding spots, and somehow Santa always knew exactly what I wanted. I remember that somehow, my skinned knees, hurt feelings, and disappointments always felt better when my mom hugged me and told me it would all be okay. I thought she was magical. Now, I know I was right.

It wasn't until I became a mom myself that I truly understood what it took to create all of that magic. The care that went into everything, the mental capacity it took to remember everything, and the sheer volume of tasks that got done in a day to keep the family happy and healthy and the house running. The tears that were cried behind closed doors—both happy and sad. It wasn't until I became a mom myself that I truly understood just how powerful my mom really was.

When did we stop appreciating just how amazing moms are? When did we stop marveling at how much they do for us? When did being a mom become something to avoid if you want to have a career or a "real life?"

I believe that mothers, as a group, are some of the strongest, most powerful people on the planet. We are also some of the most misunderstood, underestimated, and judged. The term "just a mom" gets thrown around like an insult, maternity leave is viewed as a vacation, and mothers are judged in the workforce, paid less, and given fewer opportunities for advancement. Strangers think they deserve to have an opinion on our life choices, parenting styles, bodies, and the way we dress. We are expected to look a certain way, act a certain way, and be held solely accountable for the actions of our children. All of this takes its toll and can leave us feeling defeated, worthless, and inadequate.

It's time for all that to change.

When my twins were born seven years ago, I remember someone asking me who was going to run my company. At the time, I was running my family's food manufacturing company. We manufactured pastry fillings, beverage bases, and flavourings for the bakery industry. I was in the middle of building our second plant. I can still see the look on their face when I told them "I was." The disbelief quickly gave way to judgement. The follow-up question made that judgement very even more clear. Who was going to raise my children? The response seemed obvious to me, but I answered anyways. "My husband and I will raise them, we will get childcare to help us out." That too was met with judgement and a statement along the lines of, "Children need their mother."

That conversation didn't sit well with me. I knew that my husband didn't get asked the same questions, and I didn't like the feeling I was left with—that I had to choose between being an entrepreneur and being a mom. Why couldn't I do both? Did wanting to do both make me a bad person?

The more I thought about it, the more examples I started to see of moms being told what they should do. As I looked harder, I was more frustrated with what I saw. Impossible standards, unrealistic expectations, thanklessness, and judgement. It was no wonder so many other moms I knew were stressed out, permanently tired, insecure, and unhappy. As time passed, I learned how not to internalize the judgements of others and felt called to help other moms do the same. I knew I needed to do something to help other moms see their strengths, know their enormous capabilities, and remember what it felt like to love themselves.

Most people don't know how much moms are capable of doing, even most moms. We look at the magic our moms created, the magic other moms create, and we somehow think it doesn't apply to us. We forget how strong we are—heck sometimes we even forget how smart we are. We gloss over all of the small miracles we create every single day because, for us, it's just what we do. We forget just how magical we are!

In case you don't know, or if you need reminding, here are some very simple truths about the Unicorn calibre creatures that are moms:

1. Moms always find a way. Whether it's in business, in life, for our children, or our family and friends, if a situation looks impossible, as a mom, we will find a way.

2. Moms are masters at meeting deadlines. It can often look like we have somehow hacked the space/time continuum, the number of things moms can get done in a day. If you have a deadline that needs to be met, you need a mom on the task.

3. Moms are natural leaders and negotiators. We see the people, feelings, and emotions in situations, not just the desired outcome. This allows us to get buy-in and reach compromises.

4. Moms can make something out of nothing. We don't need to

have all the "right" resources. We are creative, resourceful, and determined. Some of my best Halloween costumes came about this way.

5. Moms don't leave people behind. We raise people up, reach back and bring others with us, and in dire situations, pick them up and carry them to the end.

Looking back over this list, you will also see the characteristics and traits of successful entrepreneurs. Moms are natural entrepreneurs. Once we work past our limiting beliefs, mom guilt, and notions that being an entrepreneur might make us bad moms, we have everything it takes to be successful. The beautiful thing about entrepreneurship for moms is that it gives us the time flexibility, control, and income flexibility needed to make the rest of our magic happen, without all the stress.

I love the word MOMPRENEUR! To me, it is the equivalent of being a superhero and an entrepreneur. Not only are we able to run successful, profitable, and impactful businesses; we can do it while raising the next generation of human beings!

Over the last three years, I have had the privilege of working with and getting to know over a thousand mompreneurs, moms in business, full-time moms, and everything in between. I have concluded that not only are they the strongest, kindest, and most resilient people I have ever met, but they are also our real and true hope for a better, brighter, kinder, and more compassionate future. What the world needs now is more MOM MAGIC!

Hanna Olivas

Founder & CEO of She Rises Studios

https://www.linkedin.com/company/she-rises-studios/
https://www.instagram.com/sherisesstudios
https://www.facebook.com/sherisesstudios
www.SheRisesStudios.com

Author, Speaker, and Founder. Hanna was born and raised in Las Vegas, Nevada, and has paved her way to becoming one of the most influential women of 2022. Hanna is the co-founder of She Rises Studios and the founder of the Brave & Beautiful Blood Cancer Foundation. Her journey started in 2017 when she was first diagnosed with Multiple Myeloma, an incurable blood cancer. Now more than ever, her focus is to empower other women to become leaders because The Future is Female. She is currently traveling and speaking publicly to women to educate them on entrepreneurship, leadership, and owning the female power within.

LOVE AND COFFEE ARE MY MAGIC POWER

By Hanna Olivas

All moms have a magical power within. We kiss owies and they go away. We wipe away tears and turn them into wishes come true. We manage to be in two places at one time. We always smile even when we want to cry. We are the first ones to rise and the last to sleep. It seems we have an unending amount of energy— or so our children believe.

Being a mother is truly one of the biggest blessings of my life. I have five children ages ten to thirty. Each child is so different and requires a different magical power from me. For example, my middle and youngest daughters require my patience power. As I sit here writing this, I laugh because it's so true. My oldest son requires me to use my communication magic because he is an onion— it's one layer at a time with him. My middle son requires my sensitivity magic power because he feels everything. My oldest daughter is my diamond in the rough, and she requires my intuitive magical powers. She keeps everything in.

As I describe to you my five children and the magical powers I use, I realize no matter how old they are they will always want and need their mom and my magic.

Mom magic is real! In addition to raising children, I am a wife and grandmother. I run several successful businesses and I am a traveler. I absolutely love traveling with my family and experiencing new places and things.

Now that you have a little background on me and some of my magic powers, let me tell you where it all starts.

Every day I wake and dash to my sexy coffee machine. I bet you thought I was going to say my husband. Nope! It's coffee. The smell of my first-morning cup brings me joy. As I sit and drink the cup of what

I believe is magic; I pray, read, and meditate. I love my mornings of gratitude and solitude. Every mama needs her alone time— end of discussion!

After I finish my morning ritual, the siren sounds at approximately 7 AM. This is when we move fast. Get the kids up and ready, pack lunch, drop them off at school, and hope that this time I haven't forgotten anything.

As soon as they're off at school, I am off to run my company. Time for a different magic hat. I have a team of approximately fifteen employees and each one of them requires a mom superpower. Sometimes—or most times—it's patience and communication. I typically work nine hours a day, five days a week, and I try to do the balancing act most days. But let's be real, this requires skill and talent.

I say this because I haven't even begun to discuss my wife magic. Yup, it's a thing. My hubby whom I love dearly also needs love, attention, affection, and a wife who is present, who listens and gives understanding. One who knows his quirky ways and needs.

How the hell do I manage all this and not lose my shit one hundred times a day? Well, the truth is I do lose it or have at least one WTF moment a day! I'm not going to pretend any of this is easy because being a mama is like being a warrior at times. I'm often on the battlefield of laundry, dishes, and sticky stuff.

When the WTF moments happen, that's when I call my mama and she uses her magic to calm me. Thank God for moms right? Who knew having children was like a combo of the George Lopez Show and Family Feud?

Most days I get through with laughter and coffee. However, there are days when I need to refill my magic cup before it runs out. As a mama, we must always take care of ourselves first. Yup, you heard me! It's not being selfish, so drop the mom guilt now! Before you can help your children, you must take care of yourself. How and when is up to you! I usually take a mom day on Sundays and do whatever I want. I read, journal, and love a good facial or massage. I also highly recommend yoga because it gives you that inner silence we need most. I make sure my kids, grandkids, and hubby give me the space I need to replenish what I have used. And yes, hubby gets his alone time too. He goes fishing or golfing often, and even after so many years of marriage we still date each other with a date night or two.

There is so much that goes into being a mom, wife, and grandmother. It's never-ending. One of the greatest gifts of being a grandmother is seeing those sweet faces, spoiling them rotten, and returning them to their parents with lots of sugar and loud toys. Payback!

I believe mom magic is real, and it's incredible! To be able to create a tiny little human and watch that human go through life is one of my most cherished things in life. Seeing my youngest to oldest thrive and grow into incredible adults is so amazing. I always say, "Damn, I'm good." I raised my kids to be kind, loving, hard-working, and giving children. My grandkids are the same way. I am truly blessed beyond measure. Is it all picture-perfect? Nope. Are there days when I've wanted to give up? Yes—but I can't imagine life without them.

My mom magic comes from prayer, faith, unconditional love, and patience that never runs out.

My five tips to keep your magic cup full are simple.

1. Pray.
2. Journal.
3. Communicate -because it is key with kids.
4. Self-care.
5. Honesty -when you need help ask!

Lastly, I would also advise building your mom magic dream team. It truly takes a village to raise your children. So be open to asking for help. That's a power too; it's called vulnerability.

Ask you family and friends, church members, your therapist; heck, even your banker! Anyone who is positively vested in your child and their wellbeing.

As a mom, never be afraid to ask for help!

Remember Mama's: progress over perfection.

The only perfect mom is a happy mom!

XOXO
Hanna

Dr. Shellie Hipsky

CEO of Inspiring Lives International

https://www.instagram.com/dr.shellie/
https://twitter.com/drshelliehipsky
https://www.facebook.com/shellie.hipsky/
www.ShellieHipsky.com

Dr. Shellie Hipsky is the CEO of Inspiring Lives International, the Executive Director of the Global Sisterhood (which helps women and children around the world), and the editor-in-chief of Inspiring Lives Magazine.

In 2022, she has been heralded as: an "Empowered Woman", "Elite Business Leaders to Watch", "Most Influential Female Entrepreneurship Coach", "A Top Entrepreneur in the US", "Women Leaders to Look Up To", "Top 10 Unstoppable Women Entrepreneurs", "Top 20 Business Coaches to Watch For", "The 10 Most Influential Women Business Leaders", and "Global Woman Influencer".

The former tenured university doctoral professor, host of Empowering Women Radio and Inspiring Lives with Dr. Shellie on NBC has keynoted internationally from Passion to Profits in Hollywood to The University of Oxford in England. She has been featured on over 50 magazine covers and on all the major television networks. She frequently writes for Forbes and serves on their Expert Panel of coaches. Dr. Shellie's podcasts and vocal recording of And All That Jazz form the musical Chicago can be heard on Spotify and iTunes. She has spoken at Harvard University, her signature keynote can be seen on Amazon Prime on Speak Up!, and she recently filmed the docu-series The Making of an Entrepreneur.

An award-winning author, she wrote *Common Threads* on Inspiration, Empowerment, and Balance. Her 13th book Ball Gowns to Yoga Pants: Entrepreneurial Secrets to Create Your Dream Business and Brand is an international bestseller.

With her Global Sisterhood 501(c)(3) she collaborates with Charity Partnerships and acts of #PopUpGiving to help women around the world challenged with issues ranging from domestic violence to homelessness.

She is currently enrolling for her EmpowerU Master Class and engaging in World Class VIP coaching experiences. Dr. Shellie Hipsky is the Global Empowerment Coach who is inspiring women entrepreneurs and leaders internationally.

MOM GUILT AND A MAGIC WAND

By Dr. Shellie Hipsky

Passing off my three and 5-year-olds to their father for their very first custody weekend, I wasn't the only one crying tears of frustration. My daughter was completely confused. She didn't want to be away from her Mommy for days. She had hot tears running down her adorable rounded red face as she flailed her body away from the situation.

I wanted to pull her into me and just tell my ex that it wasn't going to happen, that they were too young to be apart from me. Them him that, although we needed to divorce, I couldn't take the separation from my "littles" for a whole weekend.

She got away from her father and scrambled under her princess bed, huddled there crying and yelling that she wasn't going. I wanted to hide with her. To seek shelter and comfort together. To take away the pain. Yet, together, we got her out from under the bed, helped to get her semi-calm, and into her father's car. I kissed their foreheads and prayed that they would get through the hard times.

Magic Wand

I wish that day, and all the other scary and frustrating mom guilt moments to come in my future, that I would have had a magic wand to wave and show me what the future would be. I would have waved my magic wand and with a simple "Bippity Boppity Boo" spell, I would have seen that it was the same mom guilt moments a decade ago (and throughout their growing years) that set the foundation for my beautifully resilient, happy, and healthy kids today as teens.

Mom guilt reared her ugly head when:

- I was a tenured education professor at a university, pumping in my office.

- I decided to strike out on my own to run my company, and I had to travel extensively for work.
- I ran a nonprofit, and because there are only so many hours in the day it took focus from the kids.
- I made time for my own self-care and health; plus, I had to tell my kids "No."
- I took care of my sick or hurt children, and I couldn't make it all better right away.
- I was just being a Mom in this messy reality of parenting!

Working Mom

I was a professor and had difficult hours to keep, as I ran from teaching early morning classes to late evening classes, often on the same day. I was up late creating lesson plans, power points, and academic journal articles with my laptop in front of me as I breastfed my babies through the nights. While I loved teaching future teachers and leaders, I felt stretched thin and exhausted. And I was guilty that I couldn't be there for my kids more of the time.

Yet, there were amazing moments with my children while being a professor of undergraduate to doctoral students. Like the time that my Jacob couldn't go to daycare, and he came to the university with me. He told people for years that he "taught at Robert Morris University" because I put him to work as a 7-year-old passing out materials and having him feel like he was an active part of the lecture. He really enjoyed making a big colorful graph and filling it in with colored markers with my student's child based on opinions of my class. Those moments made up for the time issues because he felt like he was part of something bigger than himself at a young age.

Mompreneur

When I hit "send" on my resignation letter at the university to become a full-time entrepreneur, I felt excitement, relief, and guilt. I was so excited to take my motivational media company, Inspiring Lives International, to the next level. It was showing signs of success when I started halfway through my time as a professor. I didn't realize the emotional rollercoaster of being an entrepreneur and the instability that would come from it over the years. I worried about making payroll and hitting our goals, which are always super high just because of my nature. I needed to travel often due to speaking on stages around the world, doing media such as TV shows and radio, and for photoshoots for over 55 magazine covers. I have often been on the go and had to use babysitters more than most moms.

Moving into the role of a "mompreneur" was a great thing for my kids in the long run. My children have seen first-hand my powerful unstoppable work ethic. They model this in their own lives and know the value of building something and working through the pivots and tricky times. My kids have been able to travel around the country with me on my work trips, experiencing things that they never would have if their mom wasn't the one on stage. I love that my being a mompreneur has opened doors for my children and that they have had me at all their important events such as my daughter's musical theater performances. As my son always reminds me, "Mom, you can be there. You make the schedule. You are the boss!"

The Global Sisterhood

I have dedicated a lot of my life to leading my non-profit, the Global Sisterhood, which I founded to help women and children around the world. I have spent countless hours working to help women in need. It takes time, paperwork, and woman-power to have a thriving charitable organization that touches the lives of so many women internationally. I don't take a paycheck, and there are only so many hours in the day to dedicate to the needs of other women's families while raising my own.

The Global Sisterhood has been an incredible blessing for our charity partnerships and our #PopUpGiving recipients. Countless women have been helped. Our stories of support stretch around the globe. One example is our school of entrepreneurship in Tanzania, wherein women are taught how to run and monetize their own businesses so they can support their families in Africa. Another equally impactful story is of Dr. Meena, who was a Harvard researcher who left her comfortable position in Boston to go back to her homeland of Nepal during the earthquakes. When she arrived, most of her family had passed away. She was struck by the illiteracy rate, and with the financial support of the Global Sisterhood providing running water for her town, she has taught over 85,000 women how to read and write! The stories of helping women by providing connections, education, funds, and whatever they need to fill in the gaps for their success for our Global Sisterhood are endless. My daughter, Alyssa, has been able to see and experience empowerment firsthand as she has volunteered with me to help at Treasure House Fashions to help women who have experienced homelessness and addiction feel beautiful again. She marched across the Brooklyn Bridge in NYC with me on Mother's Day as we presented Milagros Day Worldwide a check to send women who had suffered domestic violence on retreat so that they could rebuild their lives and dream again. Alyssa helped to paint a giant mural of a jungle scene on the walls of a local homeless shelter, and she continued to help as the Global Sisterhood did mom makeovers, including haircuts and outfits, so we could take family photographs with their dressed-up children in the shelter so they could have a family portrait and visualize the possibilities for the future. My daughter knows deeply the impact of volunteering. She knows how to give selflessly for the benefit of others in need. Any moments spent on my work with the Global Sisterhood are worthwhile when I see the Global Sister's success stories and when I watch my daughter become an empathic empowered woman herself, dedicated to helping others unconditionally.

"No."

So many times, over the years, I have had to tell my kids that one-word sentence that isn't always easy to say: "No." Children don't want to hear this. This word can set off tantrums and fits with the young ones and foot stomps with eye rolls as they get older. It can feel yucky to say no to our kids, especially if it is because we need to do something for ourselves, like needing to get in a workout so that we can feel sane or not buying them another toy to save our budget.

My kids survived every single "No," as will yours! Because I said the word so many times, they learned they don't need instant gratification. They understood from a young age that the word "No" is often said by parents to keep them safe. They comprehend that they can't always get what they want, but that I will provide all that they need. They get that their mom needs to spend time doing the things that keep me healthy and sane, even if that means that they may not be able to do what they originally wanted to do during that time. Most importantly, when we teach our children that we can say "No," they know that it's acceptable and appropriate to say "No" themselves when they are older to things that don't serve their needs and goals.

Can't Fix It

I recall so clearly the scream that bellowed from my toddler. I was nursing my tiny baby son at an outdoor event. My then-husband was watching Alyssa. She had scaled a gigantic blow-up bouncy-house type of slide that was set up on an asphalt parking lot. She scrambled up the slide and saw the other older kids reversing the order and going up and down the ladder instead of just getting on their butts and sliding down the slide. Unfortunately, she slipped from the top. There was no guardrail or anything to protect my baby from falling and breaking her leg. It was like time stopped. I was overwhelmed by an almost paralyzing version of mom guilt as I ran to help, but when an accident happens, try as we might, we cannot reverse time to fix it. Also, when my son was diagnosed with being on the autism spectrum and having other issues, I wished I had caught the signs sooner. And when our children get sick or we struggle through a global pandemic with our children, we simply can't make it all better quickly. All of this health-related mom guilt kept me up many nights.

Reflecting on the health issues, we made it through to the other side every time. Yes, my little 2-year-old baby girl had to wear a cast up to her hip as a toddler. Yes, both of my children have had anxiety issues and illnesses that I couldn't automatically make go away even though I wanted to. Regarding Jacob being on the autism spectrum, I was, at one time in my academic career, considered to be an expert in special education. So, when I didn't get my child early intervention services for his needs I felt a little guilty; however, he was able to be treated very inclusively by everyone because he didn't have the diagnosis. Once we did have the diagnosis we were able to make all the adaptations he needed in and out of school. And, yes, my children lived through the global pandemic of Covid-19, but we learned from that time that we could do so much from the comfort of our own homes. Both are resilient, determined, and healthy right now as I type this and for that blessing, I am so thankful. As mothers, we want to fix it all immediately, but the trials and tribulations (as much as they are struggled through at the time) do make them and us stronger.

Mom Magic

Maybe you stress over not having that perfect Instagram-worthy home or family when you see other people's highlight reels of their lives. But get real, would you want to raise a child who had a perfect life and who has no idea how to adapt to reality in adulthood? Think about the type of adults you are guiding your children towards becoming and what they truly need. I bet you are doing an amazing job!

I now realize from the perspective of being a mom to teens, the experiences that brought on the mom guilt were good for my kids. For them to grow, they couldn't have had the perfect life I had once wished for them. All of those mom-guilt moments were lessons that they had to learn to become who they are now. If I had had that magic wand to see the future, I would have seen that all the scenarios that brought on that mom guilt were the foundation for the resiliency and adaptability of mom magic.

Traci Jeske

En Vogue Stylist
Style Expert

https://www.facebook.com/envoguestylist
https://www.instagram.com/tracijeskeofficial/
http://www.envoguestylist.com/

Traci Jeske is the director of En Vogue Stylist, and a top international personal stylist, Italy's style icon and best-selling author. She helps women 50 and beyond up-level their glamour game to unapologetically create and live their best and most stylish second act ever. No stranger to wrapping up for winter, Traci was born and bred in Canada before establishing her stylish, stiletto-T sharp brand in Italy, where she has been living for the last 20 years.

Blending Italian la dolce vita with her flair for fashion and style Traci takes her personal life experiences, living in Australia, working in Dubai, London, and abroad, overcoming an eating disorder, and her experience of over 30 years in the fashion industry to have women find their unique style, be bold, stand out in a crowd looking and feeling fabulous in every season of their life.

UNAPOLOGETICALLY ME

By Traci Jeske

I am the youngest of six, so obviously—according to my older siblings—I'm the spoiled one of the bunch. I was born at a time when my father's company in the oil business took off. Life changed for my parents and money was not much of an issue when I and my closest brother were brought into the world. We traveled a lot. I have amazing memories of summers in Hawaii in the 70s, going to Disneyland, lots of fun shopping trips with my mom, and basically having whatever it was that I wanted. My parents were both fun and loving. Our home was always filled with good food, music, family, and friends.

I was always known as the super-sensitive one in the family. It did not take much to make me cry or hurt my feelings. Which, for as long as I can remember, was very hard to deal with. I always felt like I was weaker than everyone else and that something was wrong with me. I understood at a very young age that showing emotion, especially tears, was something you just didn't do, as it made everyone uncomfortable. So, I had to learn how to mask those feelings, which meant crying in my room alone and only coming out with a smile on my face. This, in turn, led me to be a complete people pleaser: since I didn't know how to deal with tears or being sad, I wanted no one around me to be sad either. I did all I could to make those around me happy, especially my mom and dad. If they weren't happy, I assumed it was my fault. It was a heavy load to carry around. This act of having to be happy all the time and not being able to express my feelings or be comforted led me to be very insecure with myself, my body, and my overall level of confidence. I labeled my soul as sensitive, weak, and not worthy. I thought that others would only like and love me if I wasn't so sensitive. So, basically, only if I was everything but me. Going through my teen years, I found comfort by numbing my emotions through food. Filling myself up with food was like a drug for me. It left me feeling satisfied. I enjoyed it, and I could eat as much or as little as I wanted. Food became my best friend— or so I thought! But eating food made me gain a lot of weight, and going through high school with such beautiful, skinny friends had my already low self-esteem go literally underground. I started to hate my body and the way I looked even more than before. Everything about me was wrong, and not being able to talk about it and having to keep it all in was leading me to my breaking point. I still remember the day I broke. I was visiting home from uni and I was extremely unhappy. It was Easter break and I was 17—I even remember what I was wearing. After another meal of eating until I was way too full, I went into the bathroom and looked at myself in the mirror. Those horrible voices overtook me so much that I purged for the very first time. Little did I know what I was putting myself into and what my life would be like for the next 23 years; the battles and demons I would have to overcome before finding freedom, inner peace, and joy.

During those years, I would binge and purge 8-9 times a day, sometimes more. I never kept anything down. My family and friends were pushed away, and in those years I had little or nothing to do with them. I was embarrassed and knew that everyone knew what I was doing once I got up from the table and went into the bathroom.I could feel their anger and frustration, and then I would have to try and make them happy again. It was much easier to be alone with no one judging me or seeing what I was doing; I wanted nothing to do with anyone. I had to keep everything so hidden, it became a job for me to fit people into my schedule on top of work, binging, and purging. No matter where I was or what I was doing I just could not wait to get home and binge and purge. It was a vicious cycle that consumed my life for far too long. But, the one thing I know probably saved me in my darkest moments was the fact that I never let myself look the part of being sick.

I always made sure I looked good. I dressed well, and I always had makeup on and my hair done because I knew that if I let that part of me go I would not be here today. If I started looking the part of being sick, then I knew it was game over for me. So, no matter what, I made sure I looked fabulous from head to toe. My style and love for fashion helped me fight one of the biggest battles of my life.

Getting my first job in retail after quitting my first year at university, I found that for the first time I was doing something that lit me up and brought me so much joy! I always loved playing dress up when I was a little girl. I was very creative and expressed myself through what I wore, and I always made sure to never wear the same look twice. Working in retail was like playing dress up all day, and helping my clients find outfits and create looks that they loved came so easy and naturally to me. I knew that somehow this was something I would be doing for the rest of my life.

At the age of 22, I had two suicide attempts. After losing my father to cancer, struggling terribly with losing him and the emotions that were inside me, and dealing with my eating disorder I decided to quit my job. I hit reset, packed my suitcases, and moved to Australia. I had no job and knew nobody there, but I had to get away. Within a month I found my apartment in Surfer's Paradise. I got a job in the fashion industry and lived there for four years. I got engaged to a man twice my age, but then when I came back to Canada to renew my visa and organize my wedding my girlfriend introduced me to this Italian man that was working in Canada at the time. To make a long story short, I never went back to Australia and never married my fiance at the time, but instead got married and moved to Italy and have been living here ever since.

At the age of 30, I gave birth to a beautiful baby boy. I had complications with my pregnancy, and my son was born premature and extremely underweight, but he soon became a strong healthy boy. I loved my boy more than anything else in the world, along with his sister, but even he was not enough to have me stop binging and purging. After putting on weight during my pregnancy, I had to lose it. I felt so uncomfortable, and the voices in my head got louder and louder. I binged and purged even more, but my body had changed and I never returned to being as thin as I was no matter how hard I tried. No one ever realized what was going on. It was much easier to hide it from everyone around me, including my husband, because I didn't look sick like I used to. By my late thirties, I was becoming tired and fed up with being sick and living like this. I loved being a mom and wanted another baby so badly, but I did not want to put my second child at risk like I did my first.

By the Grace of God and desperately wanting a little girl, I finally broke the chains of my eating disorder three months before my 38th birthday. I had tried over and over, being in and out of hospitals for years, but never managed to let it go. Three months before my 38th, I gave my heart to God completely. I gave my illness to him. I prayed and asked for forgiveness, and I know to this day it was a miracle from him. I went from purging day and night to stopping overnight and have never looked back. That was 14 years ago, and when I was 39, I gave birth to a beautiful healthy baby girl!

Being finally free of my demons, the woman that little girl dreamt to be but was too afraid and insecure to become finally came out with an explosion. Looking back now, I know my eating disorder was a way for me to keep myself hidden and small because I was afraid of my dreams. I was going against who God destined me to be, and when I got to my 40s I made a promise to myself that I would never hide again. Fear or no fear, I would do what it took to be that woman. I was stepping up to the plate, and no longer trying to make everyone around me happy but me.

Working in the fashion industry already for so many years but never being seen, I knew it was time for me to become known, be that bold woman I was, and have my center stage moment to start creating my very own successful personal styling business. Not only am I transforming women's wardrobes, but their lives as well. I want to inspire them to be all they can be and look fabulous doing so! Age is just a number and should never define how we dress, look, or feel. Working with so many women, especially in their 40s, I noticed time and time again the struggles they were having, no matter where they were from. The message I heard was that women were not feeling worthy of being seen. The fear of becoming invisible due to their age, not feeling confident, nor loving their bodies—so many things I had been through at a younger age.It was there and then that I had my ah-ha moment and I understood why I went through all I did. It was so I could serve these women through style and build up their confidence so they can stand out in a crowd and look fabulous while doing so! And thus, I had the beginning of my successful styling business and of me becoming an international style expert!

Even though I've come so far, I will always be my biggest critic. There were many times, especially at the beginning of my career, when I would let negative comments upset me. I am the type of person who wants everyone to like me, as you know, and hearing negative comments and giving value to other people's opinions and comments was a way to crush my self-esteem and my dreams at the same time. Living in a small village in Italy can have some amazing pros, but at times it can also have a lot of cons. Everyone knows you, your family, and your business, and everyone loves to talk. It seems like they are just waiting for something to go wrong. When a situation came up in my personal life, according to them everything was a result of me starting my own business because I wasn't home as much. I was neglecting my kids and family traveling around the world, or I was more worried about posting beautiful photos on Instagram than my family. Probably the most hurtful part was that this was coming from people I thought were my close friends—friends that I thought would ask me if I ever needed anything, or if they could help me. Instead, they just disappeared. The gossip made me doubt everything that I was doing and made me lose my confidence and power. After a lot of praying, meditating, journaling, and the love and support from my family and amazing REAL friends I realized that other people's opinions are not facts. I am the most important person, and the only opinions that matter are mine and my kids'. I forgave these people because I am not a person to hold grudges or be bitter. I have learnt over the years to give no value to other people's opinions or ideas, as it is a waste of time and energy. There will always be haters in the world, no matter how good you are, and often the better and bigger you get the more these kinds of people will go against you. Remember your why, live your purpose, and stay close to those who do love you and have your back no matter what.

When I think about the woman I was before starting on this adventure and the woman I am now, I always get extremely emotional. When I think about that little girl inside of me, who had a dream but was so afraid of going after it, I'm reminded that my insecurities and fear of how amazing and how big I wanted to become had me on such a self-destructive pathway to hold me back. I was hurting myself and my body every day, telling myself how ugly I was, how fat I was, how unworthy I was, what a failure I was, and that I didn't deserve to live. Then I experienced the incredible transformation into the woman I am today full of confidence and self-love. Following my dreams and stepping into that woman I was destined to be is such an incredible blessing. I thank God throughout the day for the blessing and favor he put on me and my life, because I know that if it wasn't for him I wouldn't be here today. I know I had to go through what I did to help other women and to show them that no matter what their past is, no matter where they come from, it is NEVER too late to live the life of their dreams. They can and will have their center-stage moment, and will look and feel fabulous doing so.

I can honestly say that I have never felt better than in my 50s. I felt more alive, and I loved life and myself more. I love my job, I love my business, and I love styling women. Every day is a new day because every woman and every client is unique. They are all so different, but all dream and desire to look beautiful and feel good in their skin. Yes, it is not always easy running my business. Yes, at times I felt like a horrible mother and partner for doing something for me. But my children are my number one fans, and I am determined to leave a legacy for them. They push me to do more and inspire me every day to go for whatever makes my heart sing. I am such a fulfilled and much happier woman now than I ever have been in my whole life. I have to pinch myself at times to see if I'm dreaming. I thank God each morning, afternoon, and evening for the strength and courage he has blessed me with. I have always wanted to style women and travel the world, but I never dreamt that I would style women in Dubai, London, New York, all across Italy, and many other beautiful cities. I have met so many amazing incredible women in my journey and know I have touched and changed the lives of so many of my clients and the women I have come across just as they have touched and changed mine.

Julianne Williams

Pakdavor LLC
Speaker, Author, Healthcare Consultant

https://www.facebook.com/BraveEnoughCommunity
https://www.instagram.com/brave_enough_community_/
http://linkedin.com/in/julianne-williams-1aa76917
www.juliannewilliams.com
www.conizo.com/shop

Born with a heart defect that required life-saving surgery at the age of 5, Julianne has always been resilient and tenacious.

She married her high-school sweetheart and they built a life together. Both Julianne and her husband worked on their careers for the first part of their marriage as well as traveling and completing post-graduate work.

Her husband took his life when she was 36 years of age and their children 7 and 3.

Rising in the skilled nursing sector, Julianne loved caring for the elderly. She rose to the President of the second-largest skilled nursing provider in the US with 320 locations in 21 states employing 35,000.

She recently published a book "Head Above Water," hosts a Podcast/You Tube Channel, and provides Consulting to healthcare companies.

Julianne has chaired and serves on several boards, is active in church and cultural activities.

YOU'VE GOT THE POWER: SINGLE MOM LIFE

By Julianne Williams

Growing up, I didn't dream of becoming a mom. I dreamt of the life of an executive, or a doctor, or a business owner. Most of this stemmed from the fact that I was told having children was likely not going to be a part of my life experience due to health reasons. Then my sister had a son, my nephew, and I was introduced to a form of love that was so unconditional it made me think more about how I could overcome the limitations that I was living under. The thought of not having a child was a source of sadness, and I was determined to forge a path to safely having a healthy baby.

My husband and I were married about five years when he really wanted to start our family. I spent several years "putting him off" due to fear of what might happen if I did give birth. So, I made excuses of all kinds: travel desires, post-graduate education, career promotions. After much patience, he put his foot down. We did everything "right," got married, had our advanced educations, held good paying jobs, and owned a home. So, we decided to take the plunge after getting medical evaluations and planning a course for my health during pregnancy. We were pregnant within the first month and welcomed our beautiful baby girl with abundant joy.

I have never experienced love like I did when I first met my daughter. She was perfect in every way. It was a fairytale to me; the perfect little family. Four years later, we welcomed a bouncing boy. Again, I thought we had everything planned and our future was on track to be full of dance lessons, sports, and family pictures with dogs.

I loved being a mom, and I was a great one. My education in developmental psychology was helpful in applying purposeful parenting techniques and anticipating the needs of my children. I was patient, attentive, and loving. There were established routines that included dinner time, bath time, story time, and such. Their Dad was an integral part of all of it; changed his share of diapers, picked them up from daycare and helped with them when they were sick. We were living the American dream. I had it all.

Or so I thought.

Then my husband had a mental breakdown. That lead to nine months of intense, unsuccessful treatment culminating in my husband taking his life. I was now a single, only mom. This had to be the furthest from the outcome I planned. All of a sudden, being a mother seemed a lot less magical. I had no one to rely on for help with finances, parenting tasks, or decision-making. I had no one to share those special moments with. This was definitely not how it was supposed to be.

Most of us find our lives taking a different path than we could have expected or planned, even when we did everything we could so it would turn out how we wanted. And, when this happens, it can steal the joy out of everything, including being a mother. Being a single mom can be overwhelming. It can exhaust you, wreak havoc on your self-esteem, and leave you feeling isolated. I'm here to tell you there are distinct challenges one has to overcome as a single mom, but it can be full of joy and happiness.

The first thing I had to come to terms with was being labeled. I knew what it was like to be the married mom with the husband. Now I was the single mom, the one people looked at and wondered what happened to my husband or why I had children without a spouse. I had to get used to hearing people say insensitive things, like kids who do not have fathers at home are not as successful as those who do, or that I couldn't adequately provide for the emotional needs of my children. Most of the time, these were said indirectly. Often, however, people would comment about my choices, as I did achieve my dream of becoming an executive which meant I did travel. They would comment: my "poor children" were left alone (with their grandparents or other family members) and must be so lonely. Many times, I would hear the same comments being made to my children by other parents or their children. Some classmates even teased my daughter about her father's death. If you have had these experiences, YOU are not a label, you are more than enough as a mom. Just by being you, you are magic to your children.

Financial stress can feel overwhelming when you have no one to lean on. This can create emotional strain, and steal your joy. While money is important to live, children place very little importance on wealth to gauge their happiness. If you find yourself feeling torn with pressure to "keep up with the Joneses," my young adult children have shared with me that the time and experiences we had together meant much more than the material objects I could buy them. Conversely, you should not feel guilty to pursue your dreams of a career or financial stability. The challenge of managing your financial health is one that is different from married peers. Acknowledging that additional responsibility—that it is an aspect of single parenting and that we have more to manage—validates your emotions, which can help release the isolation you may feel. Magic comes from knowing that whatever our decision about our work life, our financial situation, or as a mom, YOU have the power to create the life you want for your children.

When my children were growing up, there weren't enough hours in the day. Between work, meals, shopping, sports, school events, and the like, I sometimes struggled identifying what should be my priority. Most of the time, I was exhausted. It's hard to feel as though you are a successful parent when you are tired and pulled a million ways. Believe me when I tell you, you are doing much better than you think. As I look back, I do wonder how I made it. I also see that I did a good job of being a Mom. While I may have fallen short in some areas, there were so many in which I excelled. It's just hard to see in the moment of all of the busyness and stress. Give yourself grace to choose what you think adds the most value to the life of your family. You do not have to justify your choices to anyone—walk your own path unconcerned about the opinions of others.

Lastly, when you are on your own and parenting, there are many, many internal conversations about important decisions that our married counterparts get to discuss with support from one another. It can be difficult to make significant decisions "in your head." Your intuition and knowledge of your children's needs is strong and accurate. Trust yourself.

With all of that said, not everything about being a single, only-parent is negative. I want to encourage you that goodness lies in all circumstances.

What are the benefits I have enjoyed about being a single, only parent? There are many special things. Here are a few I have found most joyful:

- *The ability to raise my children in a conflict-free environment.* There were no fights or disagreements about how to instruct or help them. I was able to make the decisions I felt were best for them.

- *Being able to spend time with them without interference.* Evenings, vacations, and times together were special and intimate since it was just "us."

- *Special Friendships.* Other single parent girlfriends have been such a gift! Not only can you relate to the challenges, you can have so much fun together. It's truly a luxury I could not have imagined to share time and experiences with other women who gave amazing support.

Single, only-parenting may have not been the plan you envisioned for raising your children. Society has not championed those who do not fit in the proverbial "box." When that is the case, we can be made to feel like we are substandard. While parenting on your own has challenges, you should hold your head up high knowing you are offering love and opportunity to your child that is more than enough. Acknowledging the unique demands and rewards of single parenting helped me claim my power to feel confident I could provide for my children's needs. And, through that process, single parenting restored my self-worth. I encourage you to release self-doubt and affirm your value. That, my friends, is how we create mom magic.

Charissa Lauren

CEO of Charissa Lauren Collective, LLC

https://www.facebook.com/profile.php?id=100063462335238
https://www.linkedin.com/in/charissa-lauren-51737b4b/
https://www.instagram.com/charissalaurenmedia/
www.charissalaurencollective.com
www.charissalauren.com

Charissa Lauren is reputably known for her creativity and ability to connect and position professionals. She has spent over a decade as a Brand & Public Relations Consultant, starting her first business at 22. She specializes in Creative Brand Consulting and Public Positioning, exceeding her client expectations with innovative brand awareness techniques. She is passionate for entrepreneurship on every level and is working to become a multi-faceted, serial entrepreneur. Charissa has been named a finalist for the Stiletto Women in Business Award, honored by the Pittsburgh Magazine Women in Business Spotlight, a recipient of the Jefferson Award for Public Service, a nominee for Yahoo! Women Who Shine and for the Athena Young Professional Award twice. Charissa's writing has been published with Harper's Bazaar, DisFunkshion Magazine, and Maniac Magazine among many other publications. Her proudest accomplishments are her two children, in which she hopes to provide an example of hard work, passion and a devotion to travel.

DISCOVERING YOUR #MOMSTYLE: YOUR CONFIDENCE AND HAPPINESS AS A MOMPRENEUR

By Charissa Lauren

It's September 2022 and my morning is spent in New York City hustling backstage with our represented brand, Luna Selene, prepping designer Shannon Slack for her first-ever New York Fashion Week show. This is a big deal for her. This is a big deal for me! Making a client's dream come true is the most rewarding part of my job as a publicist. I live and breathe for their excitement when I deliver them that piece of good news: "You're in!" or "You got the interview!"

Here's me, enjoying the hustle and bustle of the city while taking in the moment at Sony Hall in Times Square, feeling like I finally "made it" as a publicist. The day was full of back-to-back designer shows, and the crowd buzzed with excitement. Directly after the show, I caught my flight back to Pittsburgh just in time for baths, bedtime stories, and to prep homemade playdough for my daughter's preschool. (Why is it that we always have to make homemade playdough last minute?!)

It was then that I had my 'aha moment.' This, I thought, is what the mompreneur life is about. To be at Sony Hall in the morning for fashion week, rocking designer shoes, and be back in time to tuck the babies in. What a whirlwind moment that reminded me of the reward that is being both a business owner and a mother. It's an empowering feeling that shows you that, sometimes, when the moon and the stars align just right—you really can have it all.

So what attracted me to business? Growing up, I had an independent, single mother who tirelessly worked three jobs to support us. She was the epitome of hard work and resilience, but we also struggled with not seeing her often. Most of my childhood was spent couch surfing between my dad's and my grandparents' house, and we grew close with our babysitters. When I became a mother, my goal was simple: to be there every second. Becoming an entrepreneur allowed me the flexibility to be present and active as a parent. Since my children were born, I recorded every first step, every first bite, and every first word on video, and I'll forever be grateful for those moments.

When I thought about how my life would go, I envisioned being incredibly successful as a business owner with the luxury of working from home. I wanted to be financially independent and still serve as the primary caretaker for my littles, never missing a beat. The pressure I had on myself to do it all became exhausting, especially when the pandemic hit. In 2020, I was caring for a one-year-old, expecting my second child, and scaling a rapidly growing PR company when the demand increased for digital work, throwing me into a completely overwhelming spiral. I was nursing my son what felt like around the clock while watching my 18-month-old project herself off the dining room table, and I wasn't able to do a thing about it. Meanwhile, my inbox was flooded with clients. My guilt hit. My patience ran short. I didn't feel like I was enough.

In the beginning, I thought I'd be this all-patient, mythical mom figure with homemade baby food and an endless supply of breast milk. I love being a mom, but I didn't want to lose how hard I worked to grow my name in PR. I felt tremendous guilt because I continued to try to be this perfect image of motherhood when the truth is, as a mompreneur, I am different. I felt enslaved by the long days of being stuck in a glider chair attached to a breast pump, and I missed my business. I needed to feel like me again. I was so used to a fast-paced lifestyle, and my days in that glider chair came as a culture shock. I found myself comparing myself to other moms— you know the mothers who stay at home with FOUR children (Bless them!) and are completely content? They seem to overflow with patience and grace. Why couldn't I feel that way? I waited to be a mother my whole life, but I wasn't content. I wanted more. I then learned how crucial it was to stop comparing and to discover what I have to offer as a mother.

I decided to stop stressing about the kind of mom I thought I should be and discover the kind of mom I was and embrace it. I allowed myself to pursue my dreams in business and travel. With that, my confidence blossomed as a mother. It's so important to realize that there is no one way to mom and there is no right way to mom, there is only your way. I may never be a Pinterest-perfect mother, but that doesn't mean I won't conquer mom life in my own way and with my own style of motherhood. I'll be the kind of mother that will educate my kids about the many cultures of the world through travel, instilling new perspectives along the way. I'll be the kind of mom that shows her kids the importance of following their dreams and not merely settling for a job and instilling a go-getting mindset. We will adventure. We will craft and over celebrate every occasion. We will learn about business. We will push limits and chase dreams. We will make magic and embrace every day because life is a gift.

I said in a post once, *"Do not let 'having kids' keep you from following your dreams. Follow your dreams because you have kids. And those kids need an example of what passion, hard work, and life should be."* I remind myself that being a business owner and traveler does not mean I am less of a mother. I remember traveling to Miami Swim Week in the summer of 2022 to watch our client, Gloria Ward, speak for The Wonder Woman Initiative. It was a surreal experience to start her speaking career, and I was thrilled to spend the weekend there for her support. Prior to my trip, I had a common comment from a fellow mom. She said, *"Don't you feel guilty being away from the kids all weekend?"* The truth is, I used to feel guilty, but then I learned how necessary it is for their upbringing to see me as a complete and happy woman.

The moment the child is born, we as women are reborn. Many times, we lose ourselves for a little while, only to discover that magical 2.0

version of ourselves. We don't have to mold ourselves into what we feel we should be as a mom, we discover who we are as a mom. To continue to thrive as a woman while embracing motherhood is the goal, right? Such a part of this journey is learning that who you are matters, your dreams matter, and your happiness matters! mom-ing can be a sacrifice. We constantly give and give— even more so when running a business. The truth is, the most effective way to lead is by example. This mindset helped me shake my own guilt and pushed me to pursue myself more.

To raise happy kids, we must be happy people. It's not a luxury to take care of ourselves, it's a necessity. When we are our happiest and most fulfilled selves, I truly believe our kids grow with the confidence and inspiration to become the same. I love the feeling when my daughter runs into my walk-in closet while I am changing out of my mom leggings and getting dressed up for a client show or event and says, *"Mommy, you look so pretty,"* and then she slips a pair of my shoes and sunglasses on saying, *"Look! I'm Mommy!"* Kids really do reenact what they see in you. If you're happy and successful, they will become the same. If you're not living up to your inner potential, I also believe they'll see that.

Mompreneurship is a life of chaos. It's a beautiful mess with the fulfillment of passion and purpose. Yesterday, I had the privilege to watch my client, Nolan Jae, be interviewed on air and debut his first-ever single to the radio world. It was one of the most prideful moments in my career. After the interview, I left the station to pick up my daughter from preschool. She screamed, *"Mommy!"* and ran to me with a hug. It's these days when it all makes sense. Us women, we can have it all. It may come with defeat at times, but my God, is it worth it.

Discover your mom style, and rock it. Don't let the comparison and guilt of what you feel you should be stop you from becoming all you were meant to be: as a mom, as a woman, and as a business owner. We, collectively, are raising a part of our future. It's up to us to be the example of all they can be.

Dr. Emily LeTran

CEO of Exceptional Leverage

www.linkedin.com/in/coachemilyletran
www.facebook.com/emily.letran
www.instagrm.com/coachemilyletran
www.DrEmilyLetran.com
www.ActionToWinAcademy.com

Dr Emily Letran is a serial entrepreneur, CEO of multiple dental practices, and private coach to many professionals. As an international speaker, she has been on TEDx and shared stages with countless business leaders including Sharon Lechter (Co-Author Rich Dad Poor Dad), Kevin Harrington (Shark Tank), Dr. Howard Farran (Dental Town), and Linda Miles (The Ultimate Mentor of Dentistry).

She has been featured on several magazines, Top Doctor, Dental Town, Global Woman, See Beyond as well as the media, Yahoo! Finance, Forbes, USA Today, Medium, and FOX. She is a contributing writer for several industry magazines.

Dr Letran is the Founder of Exceptional Leverage Inc., host of ACTION To WIN seminars, author of several books, and Certified Kolbe Consultant helping team grow with customized insights to boost performance. She can be reached regarding interest speaking, guest expert appearances, high performance coaching, consulting and marketing strategist by email emily@dremilyletran.com

THE MOM - THE MYTH - THE LEGEND

By Dr. Emily LeTran, *"Best Mom In The World"*

"I want to be like My Mom"

When I was 10, I hoped that my literature teacher would give us an assignment writing about moms. I wanted to describe to the world my beautiful Mom who had given us so much love and happiness for the short time she graced the earth.

I lost my Mom to cancer when I was eight. For those eight short years, I learned to love all the magic my Mom created. I remember how she was "surprised" every month when I came home with a certificate of achievement because the schools in Vietnam used to rank students monthly. I can still hear the sound of her laughter as she enlisted the whole family—and several neighbors—to help her bake moon cakes at home late into the night. To this date, almost five decades later, her students still share her stories in Facebook groups across the world.

Five years after my Mom passed away, my aunt—my dad's youngest sister—decided to escape communist Vietnam to avoid the impending draft of young men to go to war. She was taking her two kids, my 14-year-old brother, and two cousins who were 15 and 16 years old. During that one fateful night, my dad told me I needed to go with my aunt because I was "the oldest girl in the family," and I could be helpful to her. So I left my dad and 2 younger siblings behind. Our tiny fishing boat crossed the ocean in seven days, and we lived in a Malaysian refugee camp for several months. Every day, I walked on the beach looking across the water as if I could catch a glimpse of the family I left behind. I was 13 years old, and I never got to see my dad again.

When we came to the US, my aunt became mom and dad. Although she was a pharmacist back home, she took on odd jobs instead of going back to school so she could be home to take care of us. We were blessed to receive government help. With limited financial resources, I remember we shopped at chicken farms to buy whole cases of eggs, and little treats like Twinkies or ice cream became monthly specials. Now, all of us hold professional degrees, and we can order eggs a la carte at fancy restaurants!

As I grew up and became successful, I knew I wanted to be like my mom and my aunt: to give love, raise ambition, and be there for my kids.

The Myth: Mom Can Do It All

Although I was running three different dental offices, I would drive my children to school and pick them up every day around 2:45 PM. Our route from school to the babysitter's house in the afternoon often featured little remarks like "Yes Mom, I have homework," "Mom, why can't I go to my friend's playdate?" and Les Brown blasting on the radio, "You have greatness within you!"

All of my kids went to work with Mom. They filed charts by color when they could not read! They gave out forms to patients standing in line who came for Free Dentistry Day. They understood why Mom could be late when picking them up from school or driving them to Tae Kwon Do after work. They saw that at certain times of the day, Mom may drop a hat among all the ones she wears: clinician, boss, business owner, marketer, and mom.

The Myth is: Mom could do it all.

Dinner, cooked or take-out, goes on the table every night.

Holiday program, choir rehearsal, back-to-school night…Mom will be there while running her three dental offices.

Mom can even magically show up when there is a bathroom accident, broken eyeglasses, or sudden asthma attacks, at a moment's notice.

All that happened because I made myself a promise that I would be there for my kids every step of the way.

I get frustrated when my friends complain about being busy, but I do not see them at their kids' functions. They are busy growing businesses while their kids are quietly growing up.

I understand there are obligations, and I wonder why the obligations to others override the obligations to our loved ones. People share their guilt trips with me, and I often advise them to define what is most important in their life and then schedule their lives around that.

The Legend: Role Model and Support

One of the best gifts of being a mom is you almost always have an audience in the little people watching you. When you think of yourself as a role model, you watch how you present yourself, what you say, and how you act.

When my youngest son was 12, I started writing a book about my journey coming to the United States called *From Refugee To Renaissance Woman*. He shared with me that he was writing a book too. "It's a Sci-fi book, Mom," he told me, knowing that I would not ask further questions because I get lost with Sci-fi. A few weeks later, I took all three kids to a business conference. At this conference, encouraged by the loving entrepreneurs around him, he shared that the book was about teen suicide, and everyone could see right through him. It was obvious that he was writing about himself.

Realizing this at the end of the conference was a big shock to me.

Did I fail as a Mom? How come I did not see this coming?

I learned that teen bullying was very real and that my brave son was living with it for several years. We went through a long process of counseling and support from the school. I could not have kept my faith and remained strong if it were not for my mentor, who had experienced the loss of her own child. In the end, my son finished his Amazon best-seller book, *Fade Away*, endorsed by Bob Proctor. I was a proud Mom because he had developed the courage to deal with these feelings, to come through strong, and stayed resilient to finish his story.

Despite our wishes, our life journeys have dark times that test our beliefs, our faith, our competency, our values, and our nerves. I was not ready for one of my life's big tests when I was involved in a business lawsuit several years ago. If you are in business, it's just a matter of "when" you may get in a lawsuit, not "if."

This predicament could not come at a worse time. I was still in the middle of paying back several business loans, I had just bought a building with several hundred thousand dollars of tenant improvements, and I was stuck in a $10,000/month lease with no possibility of buying out. Although the lawsuit pretty much destroyed one of my businesses, during litigation I could not share that with anyone except my husband, two office managers, and my oldest daughter. I still needed to host the family parties, I still needed to give a bonus to the staff, and I still had to keep up with all the office expenses, except now it was with super tight cash flow.

The best thing that came out of that lawsuit was the realization that my husband and I no longer had the same values. He complained and picked fights over the money that "we" lost, although he was not helping me in any part of my business. He started living his own separate life in our home, cooking his own food, leaving home during the day most weekends, and only coming home at night. I was tired of the fights. I did not want him around, but I did not want my children to be part of a "divorced family" while they were in high school.

So I decided I would end the relationship when my youngest turned 18. It was a long and drawn-out journey for several years, focusing on the children and being the best mom to them while their father was a jerk. My son turned 18 during Covid, so I waited two more years. I did not want the kids in the house while we went through the process of separation.

I did not plan to set a role model as someone who put up with infidelity or incompatible values. I was setting a role model of focusing on what is most important and sticking with it despite all odds.

Divorce was not easy. I did it because I had the training and the support. I had high-performance strategies in my toolbox, I had a mentor I could lean on, I had a support group and books that I could turn to as resources, And I got peace when I walked away from my toxic relationship after 29 years of marriage. Most of all, I had my children. I overcame challenges for them. I achieved for them. One of the best compliments people tell me at conferences is "You have great kids," and I love to see my kids' sulky faces when they are told, "Your Mom is special, you know that?"

I know I raised three great young adults because they are graduating from dental school, pharmacy school, and writing school. It is not the degree. It is the character they have grown into, and they will use their skills to impact the world.

Dr. Robert Schuller said, "Tough times never last, but tough people do."

Whether you are holding your first child, losing nerve with three fighting children, or wondering if you chose the right path during dark moments like contemplating suicide, facing a lawsuit, or pondering divorce... please remember my story.

Yes, I claim "Best Mom in the World" because I am a business marketer, but we are all the best mom in the world to our children.

Never stop creating magic for them. Live up to the myth that you can do it all, and understand that to them and the people around you, you are a legend by just being YOU.

Pauline Grouette

Guided Journey Coaching & Consulting
Coach & Mentor

http://facebook.com/pauline.simundson
www.guidedjourneycoaching.ca

Leader, author, consultant, coach, and mentor, Pauline is committed to helping professional women heal and grow into their best authentic selves in their personal life and in their career! Growing up in a household where there were strong limiting beliefs, Pauline strived to become so much more than what her family was telling her she could do. All she did know as a child was what she DID NOT want to become, and that was to become any of the people holding her back! Surviving abuse, divorce, depression, bullying and harassment in the workplace as a single mother of three (8 months, 20 months and 4-year-old), now young adult children. Her mission is to help women find their voice so they can be empowered to make different decisions, that will lead them on to their most fulfilling lives. She strives to reach millions worldwide by adding to the ripple effect.

THERE IS NO CHALLENGE TOO BIG, BRING IT ON!

By Pauline Grouette

Right from conception, my subconscious brain knew that life would be challenging, so it decided to welcome any kind of survival skills that would lead to my success. These opportunities came in abundance! Lessons learned through abuse, bullying, harassment, financial hardship, divorce, and unknown paternal ties, were all significant enough to stay with me throughout my life. It took a while to understand why the universe felt I needed all these drastic lessons. My success now, as a mom and entrepreneur, came full circle to show me why they were necessary. By telling my stories, my intention is to motivate and encourage everyone that there is always a choice.

Becoming resourceful even as an infant, I sucked my finger for comfort from the cold, unemotional realities which were my childhood. Yes, I sucked my finger, not my thumb. The left index finger to be exact, and I did this until I was 12 years old! This is significant because I developed what is commonly known as buck teeth, or severely protruded maxillary incisors (12mm overjet). The bullying and name calling taught me to strengthen my outer shell, but on the inside, it still hurt. I begged my mom and stepdad for braces to make my teeth straight for many years, but they were expensive, and they said they could not afford it. Thankfully, my stepsister's teeth came in slightly crooked, so now they could find the money to get us braces. Childhood was full of challenges that forced me to be resourceful, courageous, and strong. I was determined to evolve into the leader that I knew I could be.

I learned quickly that emotions were only for the weak, and there was no way that I was going to let anyone know they hurt me. In my early 20s, I subconsciously decided to help as many people as I could so that I didn't have to feel the hurt and loneliness I grew up in. At this young age, the generational limiting beliefs were already embedded deep inside me. I wanted to date, but I told myself that I wasn't good enough, and even when I did go on a date, I would not continue dating the person due to low self-esteem and low self-worth. I was able to hide these realities by immersing myself in work and university. Then, in my senior year, something strange happened. I ended up with someone who would not take no for an answer, and I decided to throw caution to the wind and allow a small crack in that outer shell. After all, what was the worst that could happen?

Well, an abusive bipolar husband, three kids under age five, and a divorce. And then I went back to school to become a dental assistant. I needed to turn that poor decision around and get back on track. Throwing caution to the wind would never happen again! The lesson was to slow down, do the research, create a pros/cons lists, and make my children and I the number one priority!

Challenge number two, involved some of the hardest lessons I had to learn, and my motivation to keep going were my three little people that I love more than they will ever care to admit. I was a single parent for the majority of my children's lives, and a dental assistant at age 29. I wasn't even going day-by-day for the first few years, hour by hour was the norm. I was in survival mode! At one point, I was helping a family member pack and there was an unfamiliar picture of a cute little face of a child about eighteen months old, which I did not recognize. When the person said that this was my daughter, I burst into tears. I felt so ashamed. (She was eight months old when the separation started). The realities of what life was like hit me like a brick wall. I had to do better and be more present for my children! I started getting up at five a.m., before my children woke up so that I had time to exercise to get rid of the stress. I decided to take better care of my health by improving my nutrition and left survival mode! That kick in the pants told me that if I don't take care of myself, I cannot properly take care of my children. As sole provider, the judgement was all around me, provided mainly by myself. I was embarrassed, proud within limits, courageous, and determined. Finances were always tight, but I was resourceful and determined to allow my children to have as normal a life as I could provide so that they would never have to feel the way I did growing up.

I was always involved in whatever they were involved in as a way to show my love and appreciation of any help that we may have received. They were in sports like hockey (two goaltenders—if you know the cost of equipment, it is not cheap) and football, attended summer camps, and were part of the Big Brother/Big Sister organization. I ensured that they were NEVER excluded from a school trip or daycare outing due to finances. I always found a way. We shopped at thrift stores and garage sales, most sporting equipment was second hand, and we used coupons so that we would rarely pay for groceries at the regular price unless it was a special occasion. My eldest and I turned grocery shopping into a game to see how much money we could save. One time it was bulk buy day and triple airmiles; we saved close to $350 that day. It was awesome! Using collector cards was another means to save money. With the points that I collected, I was able to select Christmas or birthday gifts for items that I would not have purchased otherwise. I became PAC President for three years (two years as a member at large) and was on all their grad committees. I know my kids appreciated all that I did for them, and I know they will adopt some of those attributes when they have their own children.

Since I made such a low wage, I relied on whatever I could to be subsidized and volunteered my time however I could to compensate for it. This was how I was able to "afford" sporting equipment and register for summer camps. People, including employers, took advantage of my high standard of organization and efficiency skills. At the time, I didn't mind because I knew where my children were, they were fed, clothed, and for the most part happy. The leadership skills that I developed also set an example to my children to give back and treat others how you wish to be treated. This was always at the core of my parenting skills. It was tough but I do not regret going back to school when I did! They saw me set goals, work hard, make mistakes, and learn from those mistakes. Life was hard, and I didn't have time to let fear get in my way. I had three people relying on me. They were my motivation!

My orthodontic (braces) experience left a long-lasting impression (bad dental pun intended) on me. I always liked miniature things like dollhouses and everything that went along with them, so it felt natural for me to gravitate towards teeth. I was in love, and everyone around me knew it! I immersed myself in my dental career and was a sponge with any knowledge that came my way. I even volunteered as the toothfairy! I was fortunate enough to work with some amazing dentists, and some not so nice ones. This was challenge number three. I wore my dental passion on my sleeve. I was so grateful to have a job that I was doing janitorial duties, which were not in my scope of practice. My enthusiasm for my profession exuded everywhere, especially to my patients. I often sacrificed my time to stay late with treatment for their benefit. Throughout the later years, I developed my self confidence in an authentic manner, and finally understood my self worth. The many years that I sacrificed my worth, dealing with harassment and bullying for my career, also came full circle. My perseverance evolved my career by acquiring modules to increase my scope of practice. Actively participating in various committees encouraged my self-awareness of my dreams, which is where I am now.

My life has had amazing transitions, though especially over the last five years. I discovered paternal relations. I found my soulmate, who I have been married to for three years. My career as a dental coach, consultant, mother, single-parent, and survivor has all led me to where I am meant to be, right now, here in this moment, with you. I encourage you to believe in yourself because ultimately only you can take the actions to thrive. My final words to you would be to never feel like you are stuck in a corner or have no choice. There is always a choice! Allow yourself to embrace your courage and take those steps to reach your dreams and live your life to the fullest!

Krystylle Richardson

CEO of Life Innovation Global
Wealth Innovation Strategist, International Speaker, Best Selling
Author, Missionary, Mom

https://www.linkedin.com/in/krystylle-l-richardson-5b8903/
https://www.instagram.com/iamkrystylle/
https://www.facebook.com/KrystylleRichardson
www.KrystylleRichardson.com
www.BuildThatBiz.com

Lady Krystylle Richardson, The Wealth Innovation Strategist, The Untapped Income Coach, A Dame, The Global Ambassador of Innovation for ICN as featured in Yahoo Finance, USA Today, and numerous magazine covers. Everything she does revolves around Innovation. Her practical techniques are consistently sought after by doctors, entrepreneurs and corporations worldwide to help them manifest their inventions by utilizing her Creativity 2 CashFLOW, Innovaligy™ and Element 10™ programs. She builds up women through her movement, "Women of Impact and Innovation International" @

Womenoiii.com. Founder of Life Innovation Global TV, the home of Short Power Content, launching in 2023, the author of "The 51 Powerful Ps of Public Speaking" coming soon, she explains how bullying made her stronger. Her motto is "No Legacy Left Behind". Her goal: Reach one billion people to let them know that they have creativity and innovation inside of them to impact the world like only they can.

CELEBRATING THE INNOVATIVE CHAMPION CALLED MOM.

By Krystylle Richardson

As I thought about writing for this book, I thought about the words celebration and innovation. Anything and everything I do in my life revolve around the word innovation. In the next few paragraphs, I would like to take a journey of celebration of some of the most innovative champions in the world. They are called mothers.

Making our mark.

As a mom, we may not realize it, but we spend every day making our mark. We may have all of the ingredients for a dish that we need to make or we may not. In the latter case, we have to come up with something for our children to eat, and that takes creativity and innovation. After all, that is how some of the most interesting recipes have come about. Mothers sometimes go for trademarks and patents and have even gone on to build businesses based on their creations, recipes, household gadgets, and more. Most of them, however, just go day by day doing what they need to do to make their households work. Both instances include women as champions who should be celebrated.

I know I've made some interesting dishes (mac and cheese) and outfits in my own life. I've teased some of my daughter's friends by saying the only way that they could get the recipe is if they marry the brother of one of my sons-in-law. I love when I get a call from them while they're in the grocery store going up and down the aisles to find the ingredients because they left the paper at home or cannot find it on their phone. Good times.

Sometimes, as women and as mothers, we don't realize that we're making our mark. It is pretty magical to know that some things will go down in history just because we became a mother. Here's to all moms out there that are making their mark. Keep doing what you're doing.

Most over joyous moments.

I'm not going to lie to you, being a mother is sometimes extremely hard. There's book after book that speaks on how to raise a child, but until you have your own, you have no clue what will happen based on you and your mate's gene pool. What I can say is that some of the most joyous moments that I've had in my life had to do with being a mom and being their biggest cheerleader. This built the confidence and positive mindset they have today.

I remember various performances our children would put on in our living room. One decided to pursue engineering just like I did. She has done very well and graduated with honors and scholarships, plus she already had a job lined up before she even graduated. We are so proud of her. The other graduated from college with honors in psychology. After graduation, she went on to be a dancer that is requested to dance all over the world. She was requested by some of the Hollywood greats to go overseas and dance for their birthday parties, including a party for the princess of Monaco where she was flown first class by Christian Louboutin himself. Both daughters have good heads on their shoulders and are pursuing their dreams. Here's to the success of all of our daughters and sons.

Manufacturer of mini-mes.

How many of us have said "Oh my gosh, she is saying that just like me," about our daughters? To keep the magic going, we need to have a positive attitude and do our best to be the best version of ourselves. Our attitude to altitude ratio most likely will be translated to our children. Children do pick up what they see, even when we don't know that they're looking. I remember my own mother and miss her dearly. She had an amazing smile, was a great cook, and super great listener with great advice. I feel like my mom changed the world in her own specific way and by creating me.

So here's to a big celebration of all of the mothers giving birth to their little twins. My daughters are both entrepreneurs in their own way and have taken on some of my business mindset. I look forward to seeing what they will continue to become as they potentially become mothers themselves.

My own munchkin.

As a mother, I can only speak for myself, but sometimes it's hard to believe that a human being came out of my body. Sometimes I would make outfits for us so that we would have matching attire for church. Some manufacturers that understand the magic of being a mother have marketed outfits that can be worn by mothers and their daughters. How awesome is that? Here's to mothers and their munchkins. May you all continue to find outfits that make you feel special, pretty, and super cute.

Motherhood over miles.

One thing I have found in my experience with both my mother and my children is a mother will be a mother no matter how far away they are. I remember my mother calling to check on me because she would watch the weather channel before my domestic and international trips. I have found myself doing different kinds of checkups with my daughters too.

Sometimes I wish I could have taught them more; I wish we could have spent more time together; I wish that I could be closer to help. When we have thoughts like these, we must do our best to rely on God to give us the strength to not worry. I have to say, though, whenever I see my children's names pop up on my phone it doesn't matter what type of meeting I am in. I try to answer right away, see if they are okay, discern the tone in their voice, talk then, or call back. Being a mom is more important than any meeting.

So here's to celebrating all of the moms that do their best to balance work life and motherhood. This will continue even when the child is 70 and the mom is 95. I believe we will always have that motherly feeling.

Magical OMG mentions.

Every culture has something specific to them. In my culture, the time that has been spent hour after hour coming up with various hairstyles for my daughters was special, important, and unforgettable. We did creative braids, pigtails, beads, french rolls, hair extensions, curls, and straightening, for school, church, and everyday life.

Let's not forget the hair washing. I would always dry their hair with a towel and cover up their eyes. They would laugh and wait for me to take the towel off of their eyes and say peekaboo. I would still do the same thing even after they got older, and they would still laugh. It almost brings me to tears to write about this because of the heartfelt memories. I want to thank all of those who have come up with innovations in hair care that have helped us navigate the special times in our families with fewer tears and fewer tangles. Here's to moms with magical hair care memories. Priceless.

Miracles oh miracles.

Being able to form a child in your womb is a miracle. So is being able to raise a child these days. Still being in some semblance of a sound mind after raising children, is a miracle too. Being able to have business and financial conversations with your children and see them formulate plans to open their own businesses and make their own investment decisions after getting advice from you is a blessing and a miracle.

So, how is the magic of motherhood changing the world?

Well, let me count the ways: one meal at a time, one cheerleading boost at a time, one hairstyle at a time, one recipe at a time, one business talk at a time, one financial literacy conversation at a time, one tearful hug and "it's going to be okay" at a time, one hard truth at a time, one wish and a prayer at a time, and one smile at a time...These are all miracles.

Ladies, may your days as a mother be filled with joy, happy tears, moments of magic, moments of innovation, and moments of tremendous gratitude. I salute all mothers. You are champions of innovation. You make things work every day so that your family has a better life. God bless your life and thank you for all you do.

Keep RISING.

~Lady Krystylle

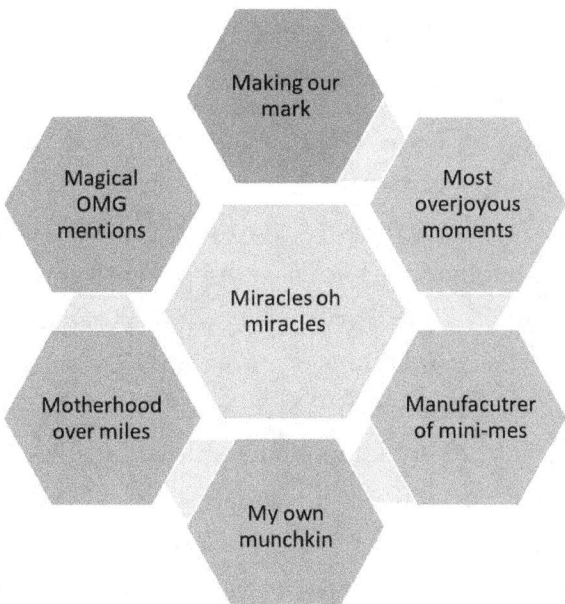

The facets of a mom illustrated

Dr. Jessica Spradley

President of Care Based Leadership

www.facebook.com/JessicaSpradley
www.instigram.com/Jessica_Spradley
www.linkedin.com/in/jessica-spradley
www.carebasedleadership.org

Dr. Jessica Spradley is the President of Care Based Leadership. Dr. Spradley has over 15 years of experience in diversity, equity, and inclusion (DEI). Her earned degrees include a Bachelor's degree in Sociology with a minor in Cultural Anthropology from The College of Wooster; a Master's degree in Sociology with a minor in Black Studies from Eastern Michigan University; and a PhD in Social Foundations of Education with a minor in Research and Measurement from The University of Toledo. In addition to her role at Care Based Leadership, Dr. Spradley has a demonstrated commitment to diversity, equity, and inclusion by training and increasing the capacity of professionals in the education, non-profit, and corporate sector. Additionally, she believes in investing in the success of women through mentoring, coaching, and sponsorship. Dr. Spradley serves on several regional and national board, but the accomplishment she is most proud of is raising two intelligent, strong, beautiful Black girls.

DOING THE BEST WITH WHAT I'VE GOT

By Dr. Jessica Spradley

"I can't do this… What if I mess up and I am the reason my kids go to therapy in 30 years?" I promise I can't count how many times this thought crossed my mind. Remembering that feeling almost a decade later on the same day one of my best friends called me a "Supermom" was surreal. It took a long time to get here, but I wouldn't trade my journey for anything. I grew up in a small town. Having lived in big cities… I now know it was a small town. My family was very blue-collar. Both of my parents worked in factories just like the other families. We didn't have a lot of money, but I went without knowing that for a while because our lives were just like the people around us, so I thought it was "normal." I was very smart, never had a ton of friends, and have been an introvert for as long as I can remember. I knew what drugs were at a pretty young age, saw many people suffer from addiction, and probably saw things I shouldn't have as a kid. In some ways, it cost me pieces of my innocence, but the spark it gave my imagination has no comparison. It allowed me to dream of the life I created.

I hated seeing my mom come home tired with body aches after work. She worked the second shift, and I vividly remember her not being able to touch us when she came home. The materials she worked with were hazardous. and to keep us safe she had to shower before touching us. That meant no immediate hugs when she walked through the door. Although I knew in my head the reason, my heart was still sad. I loved her hugs. They could make any bad day better and cure any ailment that didn't need stitches. I was convinced she had magic in her, and I knew one day I wanted to have children and a family and be the one who gave the magical hugs. As I got older, I realized that mom magic does not come with a manual. It does not have a pull-string activation, nor does it glow in the dark. To activate my magic, I had to sort through the emotional mess that I hoarded along the way.

Admitting that I had emotional baggage was not easy. It took a long time to realize that, for me, everything was connected. My past and how I envisioned my future played a pivotal role in how I lived in the present. I never saw myself as a superwoman. The stigma of the strong black woman was something I felt expected to live up to, but I wanted to be vulnerable. I wanted to have moments of fragility, and I wanted to make mistakes on my way to finding out who I was. I never felt I had that privilege. I always had a plan, and I was dead set on not failing. When I found out I was having a daughter, I immediately envisioned the perfect life for her. I would be a college professor and be available for hugs whenever she needed them! Sounded simple, but three years later when I found out I was having a second daughter, I still was not where I wanted to be. Bouts with depression and life, in general, caused me to take several breaks during my doctoral program. It took longer than I expected, but I was determined not to "fail." The day I graduated with my Ph.D., I decided to change careers. I worked so hard for my degree, I was an assistant professor at a university, but there was one thing missing. I couldn't give those magical hugs any time they were needed. The life I imagined was missing something, and for a long time I couldn't figure out what it was. I tried teaching at different times, getting my syllabi done over the summer, co-teaching courses, and doing research with other scholars so I didn't have to do all the work. I tried everything I could think of. But those magic hugs were the exact thing that was missing. I couldn't think of anything new because I didn't have the time to think. I was always looking toward what needed to be done, what needed to be addressed, what papers I had to grade, or what work in my job description needed to be done. The job I dreamed of was preventing me from living the life I imagined.

I grew up watching a majority of the adults I knew work in factory jobs. I didn't realize that there was an entire world of entrepreneurship that allowed you to work at building your own dream instead of being paid to build someone else's. I believed in the safety of a good-paying job. I wanted the security of having health care and potentially working at an organization long enough to retire. But I didn't want to give retirement hugs, I wanted to give my girls hugs now. After a ton of therapy (which I recommend for everyone), I concluded that I needed to create a new narrative of the life I was building. I watched generations of people function in a depressed state while working jobs that limited their time and freedom. I was ready to break the cycles I subconsciously adopted and create the life and job that I always dreamed about.

I would love to say that it was all sunshine and roses from there on out, but it wasn't. Being an entrepreneur is like a roller coaster that doesn't end after 60 seconds. There are a million things that need to be done, and in the building stage, I wasn't getting paid for it. There was no security, no medical insurance, and no promise of vacation. But I didn't need any of those. What I needed was the promise that when my daughters needed me and were searching for a role model, I would be there. I needed to be sure that when they needed questions answered, to be picked up from school, taken to the dentist, chaperoned by an adult, driven to the park, needed ice cream after a tough day at school, or just wanted to be loved… I would be there. I put thousands of hours into my businesses, and it does not compare to one minute that I get to spend with my girls. I traveled the world, and it does not compare to having the time to wipe one tear and give a healing hug at just the right moment.

It doesn't compare because those moments with my kids are covered with magic. I grew up thinking that the magic was in the hugs, but when I became a mom I realized it is in the desire and the will to do what is necessary to have those moments. My drive in my business is powered by being able to drive to hockey games, soccer games, practices, and gymnastics. I press the envelope on business deals because I never want to tell my children that we can't do something because we can't afford it. I don't take my foot off the gas in my personal life because my girls need me to be the best version of myself: a whole, happy, and complete person, so I can be the best mom I can be. I fight to win each day because I know that at the end of it my girls will be waiting for me to arrive feeling like my best self and still have the energy to do crafts. The power that lies within being a mom has given me the strength to start two thriving companies, actively fight depression and anxiety, survive heartbreak, and be confident that I am still living my best life. I go to sleep feeling like a boss. I wake up feeling like a boss. And I am always doing the best with what I have… and I've got MAGIC!

Sarah-Jane Layton

Soul Freedom
Soul Coach

https://www.linkedin.com/in/sarah-jane-layton-10a52545
https://www.facebook.com/sarecare
https://www.facebook.com/sarahsoulfreedom
https://www.facebook.com/groups/397137864640300/?ref=share

Sarah-Jane Layton is a full time mum to her boy Azali and in 2021 became a Mumpreneur when she decided to start her own soul aligned business online.

She chooses to live an integrous life creating family and freedom though spirituality.

Sarah-Jane empowers new mothers on their spiritual and physical journey to live a happy soulful life and create love, peace and harmony for them, their babies and families.

She has been a Tao Healing Practitioner since 2010 and empowers women, women in business and mothers to breakthrough spiritual, emotional, mental, and physical challenges to live a soulful life they love!

Sarah-Jane is passionate about empowering people to heal their relationship with money and business and she teaches soul healing techniques and offers soul guidance to create unlimited abundance.

She also mentors women to be financially independent by starting their own soul aligned business.

CREATE AND LIVE FROM YOUR HEART AND SOUL

By Sarah-Jane Layton

Part 1 – Open Your Heart and Soul and Embrace Your Magic

It has been a long and arduous journey at times, for the path is hard and bumpy. The journey of motherhood is challenging as we step into and prepare to take care of a life. I wasn't prepared for this, and many others are not ready either. I didn't have a lot of time to plan before I had a beautiful baby, Azali, who is one of the biggest blessings in my life.

For so long I felt alone and different to others, but Azali makes me feel complete and happy in my heart and soul. We have a close bond, like he's my best friend. He fills my heart with joy and love, and I am so blessed to have him in my life every day to guide and support. Now he is nearly two and a half years old, and I have journeyed with him as his full-time mum. I absolutely love taking care of him, although at times it can be exhausting. However, I wouldn't have it any other way.

As I am now an entrepreneur, I find it difficult to balance being a mum with my online business, and at times I feel completely overwhelmed with everything that I am committed to. However, I have to take one day at a time and be present in what I'm doing so that I can accomplish my commitments. Currently, my commitment is to empower other women, including women in business and mums so they can have it all and live the life of their dreams. All they have to do is stop and connect with their heart and soul to find out what is important to them and live that purpose.

I am just now opening up and sharing myself and the gifts I have to offer to the world. I offer healing and transformation to women and their families, whatever they are going through. I can assist with their emotional, mental, physical, and spiritual healing. With my work, I can guide and support you on your physical and spiritual journey and allow you to connect more deeply with your heart and soul.

Know that you are divinely guided and supported 24/7 if you ask for the support and guidance. Everyone is here for a purpose: to help others and to assist each other on this journey of life. Open your heart and soul and look within, feel what your truth is; what is it that you want to do with your life? What is it that you want to offer others? Where do you want to be by the end of 2022, and what do you want to create for 2023? Always follow your heart and soul, for they can never lead you astray. Life is meant to be lived, so don't hold back. Decide what you want and live it.

Make it happen. Book that event. Go on adventures with your child, become a big kid again, and share with others what you are creating and commit to achieving it. This is difficult for many, as they're not used to shutting off their mind chatter and connecting deeper with their heart and soul's calling. Anyone can do this. Anyone can decide to serve humanity despite the hours and work. Declare the time is now.

Part 2 – You are the Creator of Your Life

You have the power to share your heart and your soul with others. You have the gifts that are needed by humanity and Mother Earth. Today is a blessing, today is a gift of life, an opportunity to live and to create memories, and something to look back on with pride and joy. What would you love to create for yourself and others?

Time is so precious and limited, and time is also an illusion. Ask yourself: if you took away time, what would you love to do? How would you spend your days? What fills your cup— your heart and soul's calling? Make it happen. The only one that stops us is ourselves, our doubts and insecurities, and the thoughts we have about ourselves.

Connect with your heart and soul and know that you can have

anything you want for your life if you help enough people get what they want. Get a fire in your belly and find what will bring you the most love and happiness.

I have achieved much in my life, and everything I have recently done was achieved with trust and faith in my bigger vision. Life is a gift, and you need to find treasures for yourself. This is an opportunity to be honest with yourself about whether or not you're living with integrity.

Imagine the plan and implementation of your vision. How are you going to make it happen? How are you going to put the time aside? Go to your happy place; go to your heart. Close your eyes and take some deep breaths, breathing in through the mouth and out. Be free like a bird. Fly and be free. Do what makes you happy, as your happiness is important, especially when you have a family. Your happiness contains their happiness. When you are sad, your family is affected and their possibilities become limited. Know that you can have anything you want as long as you believe you are worthy and deserving. Do your utmost to take on yourself and your life and aim for the moon and stars.

Part 3 – Stand Up and Connect to Your Greatness

Open your heart to serve and to be someone of power and significance. This time is a moment in history that we will all remember: the pandemic. It has hit many hard financially, emotionally, mentally, physically, and spiritually in many ways. It has been a disruption to our everyday life. There have been many opportunities to retract from the world and limit ourselves; however, doing so is not going to empower us in life, in our career, or in our families.

Remember to release any negative thoughts about yourself. This year, last year, and 2020 were very challenging for the average person. Know that you are bigger than you think. Know that whatever you are going through is normal, is okay, and that life is a journey of discovery about oneself. Whenever you discover something about your life, or an experience that is disempowering you, know that it can be transformed and healed to love and light.

Anything is possible for you and your family as long as you know what you want and can find it in your heart to believe in yourself. You can have anything you want in life as long as you map it out and take actions towards your vision. Get yourself dressed and share what's on your heart and soul. Be free, be self expressed, be powerful, be you, and be seen. Nothing is gained from hiding and shrinking into yourself. Stand up and be proud of everything you are and everything you want. Do not back down despite the opinions of others. Live your life and be proud and confident of who you are and what you can offer, as you are unique and worth whatever you say you are.

Dream big, be bold, and learn to dance in the rain.

I am so excited about everything that I am empowered to share. You are loved and blessed beyond words and comprehension.

Part 4 – Courageously honor and respect yourself

Honor your heart, honor your soul, and do what is right for you at this moment in time. Be the leader and the inspiration for others to take a step on their spiritual journey. People feel your energy, stamina, and vitality, so ensure you have these things sorted in your own life.

Self care is a big aspect of motherhood, as there is always time that you need to honor and respect yourself so that you can offer yourself fully to yourself and others. Do you have a challenge that you are keeping to yourself? Know that a problem shared is a problem halved. Life is good. Take daily action for yourself and others, truly live in the moment and create your life with excitement!

Open your heart and soul to have the freedom to be authentic about what you need and ask for help. Help is always available, step forward into your commitment and commit to what you say you're going to do.

This is my message for you on this day.

Shonie Short

These Artful Hours
Therapeutic Arts Coach

www.instagram.com/theseartfulhours
www.theseartfulhours.com
https://these-artful-hours-1.heymarvelous.com/

Shonie Short is a professional artist, registered therapeutic arts coach and certified NLP practitioner with over ten years of experience leading creative workshops in health, care and community settings.

Her work has been featured in international galleries, festivals and journals and she has spoken to global audiences, sharing a simple message, art is everywhere and for everyone.

Shonie holds two Masters degrees and is currently leading a PhD research team investigating how art can be used to create spaces of care for women.

Shonie set up her first company in 2009 to deliver extraordinary arts experiences in ordinary settings, and it has been growing ever since. In 2022 she launched a new venture, These Artful Hours, an online creative wellbeing studio that focuses on using therapeutic arts to give mothers the tools to relieve stress and anxiety symptoms for themselves and their children, through 1-on-1 coaching and group workshops.

UNLEASH YOUR CREATIVE GODDESS

By Shonie Short

"I'm just not a creative person"… If I had a penny for every time I've heard that!

I've spent the last decade leading gentle and joyful art workshops for women just like you in health, care, and community settings, and I've SEEN the healing and growth that happens when women create. And yet, so many of us cut ourselves off from our creative side because we are too busy, we aren't talented enough, or we'll never be professional artists or art experts. So what's the point, right? We've lost touch with the little girl who spent hours choosing crayons and drawing pictures, making up wild and wonderful stories, singing and dancing with or without an audience and never once worrying about whether she was good enough.

I was that little girl, I loved art and messy play, and escaping into worlds of my imagination. But, when it came to the rigid structure of the education system and the harsh judgement of adults, just loving something wasn't enough of a reason to nurture it. With no particular skill in drawing or painting, I wasn't allowed to take art classes in high school, and I was directed towards more 'suitable' subjects in which I was likely to achieve higher grades. Oh well, I thought, I guess I'm just not good enough to be an artist. And I put those crayons and stories and songs back in a box marked childhood toys.

When did you stop drawing for fun? A friend of mine who teaches adult drawing classes claims she can tell in the very first lesson exactly what age a student was when they gave up drawing as a playful activity because their skills and style have never developed beyond that stage. How could they, without regular practise? What's incredible is that so many of her students share the same story: they were told in school that they weren't good enough, playtime is over, put the pencils away. And yet, here they are back in school with their love of drawing reignited as an adult.

As for me, I graduated in a non-arts subject and built a successful career managing the logistics of multi-million-pound public art projects. It was a wonderful job in so many ways, but I always felt I was sitting on the wrong side of the table. I found myself in meeting after meeting wishing I could create the art instead of the budgets and marketing strategies. I picked up brochures for night classes in drawing, writing, and photography, but somehow never found the time to go. I took up craft hobbies every other weekend but gave them up just as easily when I wasn't immediately brilliant. The lesson I remembered from my younger days was that if I was an artist, I would be effortlessly brilliant.

Putting my creative dreams aside, I threw myself into raising my three sons, and for a time that was more than enough to keep me occupied. But, when my youngest son started school, the artist inside me sensed an opportunity to be heard. My son came home one day with a simple homework task, "What do you want to be when you grow up?" As we talked it through, I realized I was in no position to encourage my children to follow their dreams if I wasn't prepared to demonstrate it for them. How could I inspire them if I couldn't inspire myself? I marched myself down to my local art school and persuaded the tutors through sheer force of passion that, without any relevant qualifications or even a portfolio, they needed me on their course.

Since then, I have achieved two master's degrees, my art has been exhibited and published in galleries and museums nationally and internationally, and I make a full-time living from art. It's what I do, it's who I am. But the work that really lights me up—the work that makes me jump out of bed in the morning—is helping women like me who were taught to believe that they aren't creative or artistic to prove everybody wrong. Because here's what I've learned: creativity is a muscle. We all have it, no exceptions, and the more you use it, the stronger it gets.

I meet one category of women in particular who are most likely to tell me they aren't creative before immediately wowing me with their creativity, and they are… moms! When you think about it, this makes absolute sense. The very definition of creativity is to bring something new into the world, and to be artistic is to have the ability to create something beautiful or meaningful. Look at your children. Look what you made. You are amazing! As a mother, you are naturally channelling the divine creative, because every day you are shaping something more precious than marble or gold.

If you need more proof, think about how many times in the last month you creatively solved a problem. Maybe you made an incredible new meal using only leftovers or stopped a tantrum in its tracks by doing something unexpected. Perhaps you pulled together a last-minute costume or school project using supplies already in the house. Just this week, how many times did you see things from your child's perspective and adapt accordingly? These skills are the foundation of creativity, and when it comes to artistic skills… well, already today I have been a storyteller, fashion stylist, chef, interior designer, event planner, and photographer and it's not even noon.

We are not only creative moms, we are also creative muses, inspiring our children with all that we say and do. Every child is an artist, and you are their first and most significant source of inspiration.

So, imagine for a moment that your child has brought you a drawing. Do you look at it at think, "Oh dear, this isn't a great piece of art?" Of course not! Perhaps the figures are as big as the houses, or all the colors have mixed into an ugly brown splodge, but that's not what you see. You see the joy and the love that has gone into creating it, you see the pride in your child's eyes in their creation, and you recognise that what you have in your hands is beautiful.

What would it feel like if you gave yourself that same permission? If you allowed yourself to make something, anything, for the pure joy of it? If you let your childish delight in choosing a crayon to override your adult inner critic, you might just discover that you've been a creative goddess all along.

Maybe you're reading this thinking: Okay, she wants more women to connect to their creativity, that's not a terrible mission, but it's not the most important thing going on in the world right now. But here's the thing, when women step into their creative power there is nothing they can't do. Imagine a whole movement of these women. Imagine the creative solutions they could find to any and every problem. Imagine the creative energy they could bring to all fields of life. That's what inspires me to get up in the morning.

Women like you, moms like you, can and will make a difference. When we unleash our inner creative goddess and step into our creative power, we see the truth—that creativity is not simply a nice thing to have. It is fundamental to what makes us human, and it is how we will leave our mark on the world. The slogan of my company, These Artful Hours, is "beauty, joy, purpose" —because these are the things that make life worth living, and these are the doors that creativity can open.

So, next time you find yourself about to say, "I'm just not a creative person," or you hear another mom saying, "No I'm not artistic," remember that creativity is a form of practical magic that belongs to everyone. As acclaimed artist Ai Weiwei says:

"Creativity is part of human nature. It can only be untaught."

You are a mom. You are a creative goddess. Go create the world you want your children to live in.

Nessa Lovell

Art by Nessa
Intuitive Artist & Colour Therapist

https://www.linkedin.com/in/nessa-lovell/
www.facebook.com/nessalovellart
www.instagram.com/nessalovellart
www.nessalovell.com
https://nessalovell.com/landing/colour-meanings

Nessa Lovell is an artist, intuitive, healer, guide, mother and wife from the beautiful Yass Valley, in NSW, Australia.

Nessa's main theme in her life has been magic - seeking it, finding it, experiencing it, creating it. Throughout her journey as a young, solo Mum to a face painting fairy, to an artist who weaves magic into her artworks, Nessa has sought to imbue her life and her offerings with a sense of wonder, magic and transformation.

Currently Nessa uses her knowledge and experience of energetic and emotional clearing techniques, essential oils, colour therapy, spiritual healing and energy work to create beautiful abstract artworks brimming with their own unique magic. Once created, Nessa can 'read' these artworks - taking their new owners on a journey through the colours and patterns and how they relate to their lives.

Nessa creates artworks with collective messages daily so follow her to discover these magical pieces.

FINDING MY FAIRY DUST

By Nessa Lovell

As I sit here writing this, I am surrounded by the creative mess of my home art studio—countless bottles of brightly-hued inks, essential oil blends, papers and canvases, crystals, plants, and piles of my artwork—and my heart is full. Full of gratitude for the glorious artwork that I am honoured to birth into the world daily, and all the support of my friends, family, and husband over the years that has made this possible. Full of pride for the dedication and commitment that I have given to practising my craft, and being willing to do the work on myself as well. Above all, perhaps, is the inner glow and knowledge that I have recently discovered that confirms I AM worthy of all this.

I don't know about you, but I've had an internal battle with myself for years around this very subject. On some level, because I have always had good people in my life to keep me on track—a life thus far void of overwhelming sadness, loss, abuse, or tragic events—I felt that I somehow didn't deserve to have success. I had a subconscious belief running, I felt like there was only a finite amount of 'success' (whatever that means) to share around, and that I should step back and allow those that have earned it through suffering to have it instead.

Of course, success isn't like that. It comes to those who choose to seek it, do the internal work on themselves to prevent the sabotages that tend to accompany it, and keep showing up. I truly believe that ALL of us can be successful in our lives, and it's not about 'earning' anything, but taking ownership of ourselves and our behaviour is what will get us there. That, of course, is the crux of my story (or this one anyway), so let me explain.

For as long as I can remember, I have felt like I was put here for a reason. I had a 'Life Purpose,' but I had no idea what it was. Somewhere along the way, I picked up the idea that I was here to change the world, and for years I felt this desperate sense of failure because I didn't know how that would happen, what it would look like, or why it was all taking me so long. It was overwhelming.

At 43 I've had an interesting life, but I've only just started. I grew up in a little town on a 5-acre property with my family. Baking hot Australian summers were spent running around the garden with my bestie, catching Christmas beetles out of the trees, or making whirlpools in our little swimming pool. There were evenings when we turned off the lights to watch the lightning or the stars. Afternoons were spent wandering around the garden with Mum telling me the names of the plants, and heating saucepans of water on the stove to have baths filled with handfuls of lemon balm.

I was always creative and fascinated by all things mystical and magical. I decided early on that I wanted to know how the human mind worked, and I have spent a lifetime learning about things like hypnosis, tapping, spiritual healing, and various ways to understand and reprogram beliefs. I went to psychic fairs whenever I could, as I had a deep need to understand that which cannot be understood by our human brains—energy, spiritual healing, and what happens when we die.

A week before my 20th birthday I discovered I was pregnant with my daughter. I've always been an "everything happens for a reason" person, so even though it was all very unexpected I decided to roll with it (or her I should say) and see where this new adventure would take me. The next few years were a bit of a rollercoaster—living with my parents, then my partner, then my sister, and then just me and my daughter, and then my son too. Postnatal depression, relationship breakdowns, loneliness, exhaustion, feeding issues. I was a sole parent for eight years. Had it not been for the support of my family during those years, I'm not sure how we would have lived—and I have endless gratitude for how they helped. Living on government benefits to care for your children does not allow much room for anything but necessities, and even with our own home (thanks Mum and Dad) money was tight. And yet, through it all, I had an unbreakable bond with my kids (my second child was born when I was 23), and I am proud to say they have grown into beautiful adults that have their own positive impact on the world around them.

During all this time, I kept learning, kept searching for my purpose, and volunteered wherever I could to "earn" my benefits. I created a program to teach young people about the realities of teenage parenthood. I completed a Diploma in Community Development. I was a "big sister" in a community program. I started my own business as a face painting fairy and children's entertainer. I started working full-time at a local school with kids from military families. At 31, I was married to my now husband, and a few months later our little family posted off interstate. We lived in four states in six years, and not only did I take my business with me, but I also took on more work or volunteering roles wherever we went, as well as general Mum duties.

In my 30s, I started doing lots of personal development work. I had another baby, had major surgery, attempted a university degree, face painted for free at the Children's Hospital every week, and donated eggs.

My business had been an obsession for me for years. I was subconsciously defining my worth by how hard I worked, how much time I gave to others, and how much I earned (which wasn't much), and losing sight of the important things in the process. When my youngest was a toddler, I finally decided it was time to let my fairy business go. I felt like I had failed—so much time away from my family and still no money to show for it—but, of course, I jumped straight into the next project (essential oils and my art). This time I worked myself to the point of pneumonia. I knew something had to change, but I wasn't sure how or what.

There was a defining moment for me one day when I was doing some inner work, and I realized I had been running on this program of 'I am unwanted' for most of my life (this wasn't from my family). This belief had led me to associate my worth with what I did for others—and had me exhausting myself trying to be everything for everyone. The more I did for others, the more praise I received, and I craved that external validation because I wasn't giving it to myself. I had always believed I was just doing it all because I loved helping others (and I do), but hiding underneath that was the real reason I did so much. I did it to feel loved, wanted, needed, and useful because somewhere inside me my ego kept telling me I wasn't.

So, it was back to the drawing board. I decided to stop doing what I saw other people succeeding at and do what lit me up instead. I was tired of playing small. I started weaving together my various interests— combining art and oils with energy work and emotional clearing. I worked on my old money stories that said that money causes arguments. I finally acknowledged that my artworks are GORGEOUS and that I am brilliant at what I do. I stepped up. I invested in a photo shoot and business coaching. Then my coach helped me to see that MY unique magic, my fairy dust, is the one thing I've always wanted to do but been terrified of failing at. When I started telling my people the truth—that my artworks have magic and energy and transformation woven into them, and that I can read the paintings and work 1:1 with my clients—something shifted. I suddenly felt in alignment. The opportunities were sprouting everywhere. I put my prices up for the first time in ages and had no qualms about doing it. I SEE myself. I feel confident (and yes, still a little terrified).

It has taken 43 years to find my 'Life Purpose,' and it isn't a career— it's just being myself and showing others it's safe to be themselves too.

Over half that as a mother to three children, marriage, multiple house moves, various business ventures, many jobs, volunteering, studying, LOTS of inner work, learning, experiencing, growing.... and I have no doubt that what I do will keep evolving. I don't believe in stagnation. I still believe that everything happens for a reason and that every stepping stone along the way has brought me here. I found my fairy dust, and it was inside all along.

Cathy Callahan

Maxwell Leadership
Certified Coach, Teacher, Trainer and Speaker

www.facebook.com/cathykteach
www.instagram.com/heysweetmomma
https://www.linkedin.com/in/cathycallahan/
www.pcatu.com
www.socialsaleschool.com

Cathy Callahan is a Business Coach who helps female entrepreneurs grow and scale businesses through simple systems founded on purpose and impact.

HEY SWEET MOMMA

By Cathy Callahan

What is stopping you from going from where you are to where you want to be? How many times have you wanted to start that business or do that next best thing for your business, but something stopped you? Maybe it's that full to-do list, and you keep coming last on it. Or, maybe you aren't really sure what exactly you should be doing, so you don't start. Or, you do start and you get interrupted, or you interrupt yourself…

Hey sweet momma, I get you. I am you. There are so many things you are balancing. On top of the mom duties, you are also learning how to build your business and maybe even discovering why you want to in the first place.

Let's go back to some new mom moments. Allow me to take you on a business journey that should feel quite familiar. Think back to that new baby, how often did you really feel like getting up in the middle of the night? How often did you really feel like doing all the things that it's taking to raise those kids? What pushes you to do it?

Well, congrats! You have birthed a different kind of baby. This is your business baby.

Since I have a few moments with you in this book, my goal is to inspire you, encourage you, relate to you, and give you some action steps that you can take so that you can go from where you are to where you want to be.

As a single midwest momma to all boys, with a background in teaching, and lots of years as a mompreneur, very little of what I do has been because the timing was right. There is always a reason NOT do something, but the shift I hope to help you have is why you SHOULD do the darn thing. I hope to provide you with some parallels to what helped me to be successful and helped me get past my stinking thinking and continually wake up every single day and take action.

So, what's the motivation? What's behind you wanting to build a business or the business you already started? Are you passionate about what you are doing? Do you have goals set? What will it feel like to achieve these goals? Who is limiting you from achieving these goals?

I first decided to start my own business during my 5th year as a kindergarten teacher. I always wanted to be a teacher growing up. I didn't have to think about it, I just knew. I got my BS & MS in early childhood education and became a kindergarten teacher, and I absolutely loved it. Then, I had my own child. Before he was even born, I started thinking that I wanted to do something else with my career. I wanted time freedom and choices I didn't have as an employee, and I didn't want my income to be capped. I could get a small raise for each continued year I taught, but that was it. It didn't matter if I wanted to work harder, or be more creative, or go the extra mile; I wasn't going to get paid for that.

I decided to take a leave of absence when my oldest son was 17 months old. During that time, I was invited to a home party. I remember what I thought about the girl presenting at first. I thought, "Isn't that so cute for her and her little bored stay at home mom business," but it didn't take me long to realize that I was making assumptions. I really did want something different for myself, so I decided to do something different. I started building a home-based business, and traveling two to three times a week doing in-home spa parties.

I resigned from teaching six months later, and I spent the next six years learning what it really takes to build a business, balancing being a mom, and finding a part of myself that I didn't even know was there. Building a business was something that was for me! I had to do the hard work, step out of my comfort zone, and do something different.

It was scary, too!

Because it is so new, your business baby will come with a lot of really neat experiences, challenges, and obstacles—and I still haven't found a business manual that addresses every single scenario I have encountered. I still haven't found a parenting manual that does that either, but I have learned a lot of things that helped me in the journey.

Through my years of teaching, network marketing, taking over the family home care agency after losing my mother, and then returning to network marketing after selling the family business, I found my way into business coaching. I work with online entrepreneurs and help them discover their purpose and create their business plan.

I surveyed my students and I asked what I should write my chapter about. What would make an impact on the readers? What would give them something to think back on and say, "Hey, I remember reading that chapter and it was a changing moment for me."

So, allow me to share my top 10 tips for you as you move forward raising your business baby.

1. This is your journey, no one else's. Stop comparing now; it's not worth the mental energy. As John Maxwell says: focus on COMPLETING people, not COMPETING with them. Hey sweet momma, you can do anything… You really can! In 2012, after losing my mother, her home was being foreclosed. I rebuilt the family business out of a garage stall in a home that was going to be taken by the bank. I had a HUGE reason to do it. I stood around and thought, "How can I compete with these big businesses with pretty signs, marketing materials, and actual office buildings?" That's when I learned to serve people, give value, create relationships, and set myself apart by going the extra mile.

2. Next, it's not going to be easy. But hey, you're a mom. You know how to do hard things. Lay out your goals, create your plan, and get an action plan together. Focus on the daily to-dos and one day you will look back on your business, just like you can with your child, and say, "Wow, all that work paid off."

3. Most people quit— Don't be a quitter. Do you want your business to work? Then you have got to work on your business. Don't quit.

4. This is not about you. You might think it's about you, but it's about your family, your bills, your business, and your impact. The truth is that if you want to build a successful business, you're going to have to shift the focus to others. Use WIIFT: What's in it for them? Start thinking about how you can help others: what needs they have, what problems you can solve, and how you can bring value to others. By shifting the focus, you'll let go of all the things we do to ourselves when we stress out over not getting results or when someone does not approve of what we're doing. Maybe a customer isn't buying when they said they were going to, or somebody returning a product or was unhappy with your service. Listen, empathize, and don't take things personally.

5. Done is better than perfect. One of my past coaches gave me this thought process, and it's one that I have paid forward to so many of my students because it stuck. Are you stuck in procrastination? Is it really fear that's holding you back? Turn your excuses into your reasons, and go take imperfect action.

6. You can monetize anything. At the time I am writing this chapter, I just did a Facebook post on fake freckles and rouge booty pants. I mean, who sat around thinking of these things? Yet, they're taking over the internet. So, if you're sitting there

thinking: "Would people pay for that?" There is only one way to find out. The bigger question is: would it bring you joy to do that thing? Quit trying to sell what you think people will buy, and start serving and creating your mission. What are you passionate about? What brings you joy? What could you talk about all day long? What would you wake up and do with a happy heart no matter what? Even if the kids are screaming. Even if things come out differently than you planned. Even if you get divorced. Even if a family member dies. Even if people question you. What will you keep doing anyway? This is what you should be doing.

7. If you're trying to build on social media, let me give you my biggest piece of advice. Start being you. Be open, honest, and vulnerable. Offer hope and be a solution. Don't be afraid to be direct. If you have conviction you don't have to be convincing.

8. Hire help if you need it. What is taking up all of your time right now that if you moved it off of your list, you would have time to do what you need to do in your business? Hey sweet momma, let go of the guilt. Hire the housecleaner or babysitter. Swap time with a friend if you need to.

9. Invest. It takes time and money to grow a business. When I didn't have money, I gave more time. When I didn't have time, I used money to hire help or invest in business tools or training that could help me fast track my results. If you don't have time or money, do you want it to always be that way? Let this be the fuel for really going after your business dreams!

10. Walk in faith and listen to your heart. Don't let your head get in the way. Whoever said you can't doesn't matter. What you say about you matters.

Let me leave you with this: Three years from now, where do you want to be? Can you see your future self? What do you need to do right now to become that future person? What will your life look like three years from now if you keep doing what you're doing?

Bite-size pieces, momma. The baby didn't just come out. It didn't just start walking. And nothing you've ever done in your life was accomplished overnight. So, stop overthinking this one. What small action steps do you need to take every single day? The first one, write yourself that letter. Get that pen out. Imagine it's three years from now and we have not spoken in between. What does your life look like? You get to write the story. No stalling or excuses. Not later— Right now. Write that letter. And if you're so inclined, go ahead and find me on social media, and share that letter. I cannot wait to celebrate with you.

Xoxo Cathy

Shavon Leach

Forever Open Journal & Notebook Collection
Owner and Founder

www.facebook.com/foreveropenjn
www.instagram.com/foreveropenjn
www.linked.com/shavonleach
www.forever-open.com

Dr. Shavon Leach is a mother, wife, entrepreneur, leadership development consultant, a creative, and social justice activist.

Dr. Leach has a BA in Biology and in Leadership Studies, a graduate certificate in HRM, an MS in Organizational Leadership, and an Educational Doctorate in Organizational Leadership. With a passion for helping the community, Dr. Leach uses her expertise to help individuals become self-aware leaders. She uses her creativity to increase community engagement and educate the community on laws and policies that impact their lives.

Dr. Leach wholeheartedly believes in people and their power to build community strength.

Dr. Leach created Forever Open Journal & Notebook Collection LLC to give people a brave space to reveal their inner truths, connect with themselves, and build the inner confidence needed to become a better version of themselves.

MOMMY, ENTREPRENEUR ME

By Shavon Leach

I decided I wanted to start my business a month before I gave birth to my second son. I had no plan and was completely unsure of how I was going to do it all with a growing family while in school and working. I knew it was important to me to build a business that was in tune with some of my goals as a mother. I wanted my children to be open, brave, and confident in their purpose. I eventually chose Forever Open Journal & Notebook Collection because I love to write and journal, and being able to express myself helped me. My business does more than get people to write. Forever Open helps people open up who they are, gives people a place for their deepest thoughts, encourages peoples' spirits and builds a strong mindset, gives people a place to express themselves, and helps people be more confident in who they are and who they are meant to be. Most importantly, Forever Open helps people step into their potential. These were all things I wanted to do for my children as well. So, a stationery business made sense.

Much of the work I do for my business requires late nights. As moms, 99.999999% of the time we are the last ones to go to bed. After cleaning up from dinner, putting the kids to bed, cleaning up the house, and all the hidden crumbs, I am finally ready for bed. But in actuality, I have content to write, journals to edit, notebooks to design, posts to plan, emails to develop, orders to fill, et cetera. I remember countless times of getting done with work, cooking dinner, getting the children ready for bed, and being so tired, only to realize that my day was far from over. I still have articles to read, citations to correct, and papers to submit for class. Then, I had to prepare for vendor events and other business matters that I couldn't put off anymore. I was up all night, especially when the twins didn't sleep through the night.

There were times when I wanted to cry. So, I did.

That's okay. Cry, mommy, and keep going.

The ugly truth about being a mom and an entrepreneur is it's not always fun. Let's be transparent for a moment. There are times when we don't want to be Mommy or run a business. I am telling you that it is OKAY! Let's remove the stigma attached to saying these things. Mommy, Mom, Mother, and Ma, it is okay to feel this way, but it is not okay to stay there.

Our lives as moms and entrepreneurs are needed. You are needed. There is an impact that you are meant to make that only you can make. There are lives specially assigned to you who you are meant to help, heal, guide, and push into greatness. When you give up on yourself, you give up on them. Yes, Mommy, I know you are tired. Yes, Mom, I know no one liked your post today, and the children are not behaving. Yes, Mother, I know those closest to you are not supporting you. In fact, some of them are rooting for your failure. Yes, Ma, I know people are trying to work against you.

Keep going!

Keep going!

Keep going!

I know it's hard, but you can do it.

To keep me going, these four things have helped me:

1. Find your identity in God — Knowing who you are in God gives you confidence and self-awareness to live out your purpose. Knowing who you are in God helps you to understand your journey. When I found my identity in God, I realized he created me as exactly who he needed me to be. I realized I am on my path, and there was no need to question

it. God has given me everything I need. I just needed to access it. Through Him, I have the strength, creativity, and the power to be an excellent mother, business owner, and more.

2. Make sure your goals and focus are aligned — Making sure your goals align with your focus as a business owner will help you stay on track and remove a lot of stress so that you don't take time away from your family. As a mom and an entrepreneur, I wanted to help others, help my children, and serve God. Keeping these objectives in mind helps me continuously build and grow with purpose and on purpose. In addition to wanting my children to grow into well-rounded adults, I want to leave them with a legacy of helping people step into their potential through God.

3. Re-energize — Taking time for yourself to reset gives you the opportunity to breathe and clear your mind, refresh your energy, and give you a confidence boost. Being a mom and an entrepreneur and wearing multiple hats, I get tired, overwhelmed, burnt out, and stuck. It is important to take some time for myself. Something as simple as taking a nap or having alone time helps me to reset. I also make time for counseling. There is no shame in needing a break or in getting help. Both are important, and both allow me to move forward.

4. Understand your impact will be great — You started your business to make an impact. You need to know that you are going to help someone, you are helping someone, and that their lives won't ever be the same. We often get frustrated when our efforts as a mom and entrepreneur seem to be going nowhere. Being able to see the fruits of our labor takes time. Building a positive impact takes time. Raising a family takes time. I know that as long as I stay on track and move with God, my children and my business will be great.

You have to remember to give yourself grace. You have to realize that you are good enough. You do not have to pretend to be (or try to be) Superwoman. Superwoman has superhuman abilities. Superwoman is not real. You are real, and the impact tied to your name is super. It is time to stop comparing yourself to an unrealistic character. It is time to start showing up as the magical woman you are. I believe in you. I believe in the positive impact you will make. I believe in your strength. I believe in your path. I believe in your capabilities. I believe in you because I know the amazing things that Mommies, Moms, Mothers, and Ma's are capable of doing. I am in your corner, and I am cheering for you.

It took a long time to see my magic and believe in myself. I understand the struggle. I know what it is like to look in the mirror and not see an effective mom or business owner. Once I learned how to continuously implement the four points I mentioned above, I was able to give myself grace.

I wish there was a switch to flip and say that you have "it." But the truth is, you have to make it happen. Wake up every day ready to tackle being a mom and running a business. Wake up every day ready to live out your purpose; not someone else's or like anyone else's.

Our journey as a mother and an entrepreneur is magical. Not because we have everything in place and not because we are reaching all of our goals, but because we are showing up as our imperfect selves and positively impacting others.

That's mom magic!

Jennifer Lara

Founder of Becoming a Wealthy Lady Boss
Lara Financial

https://www.linkedin.com/in/jenniferlara509/
https://www.facebook.com/iamjenlara
https://www.instagram.com/iamjenlara/
https://www.iamjenlara.com/

Jennifer is a Financial Services Broker, Bestselling Author, Money Education Coach, Entrepreneur, Speaker, and a busy momma passionate about educating ambitious mompreneurs and woman of color on financial growth.

She is enthusiastic about giving back to the community and is recognized for her commitment to connecting passionate female entrepreneurs through hosting networking events and retreats for women in business to collaborate and build true authentic relationships.

BECOMING A WEALTHY BOSS MOM

By Jennifer Lara

"Being a mom has made me so tired. And so happy." —Tina Fey

A mother is a nurturer and unconditional love-giver, therapist, doctor, and discipliner. Mothers are magical. We can do everything. We even own businesses! We are dreamers, and we have everything within ourselves to change the world. Patience, resilience, and adaptability are just some of the many qualities it takes to be a great leader—and who encompasses those qualities better than mommas?

Through my mompreneur journey, I have learned that in business and motherhood it's all about focusing on the things that will expand your life in a way that will bring you and those around you joy, wellness, and fulfillment. That is why I am writing this to remind you that you are unique, valuable, skillful, and worthy of even the wildest dreams you hold in your heart. Most of all, you can transform and rise above whatever hurdles you come across in your mompreneur journey!

As the Founder of **Becoming A Wealthy Lady Boss**—the movement that empowers women to take control of their financial future so they can live a life of freedom, choice, wellness, and fulfillment, I know first-hand what it's like to start something from scratch; to have big dreams and an ambitious vision, and what the process is like bringing that vision to reality all while being a stay-at-home mom! That is why I am passionate about collaborating with other badass, mission-driven women to help, encourage, and guide them towards reaching their ultimate financial and life goals.

You see me now as *Jen* the *Latina Money Education Coach*, but there was a time when I didn't know how to prioritize myself and my finances. As a first-gen entrepreneur and woman of color, I had zero education when it came to financial literacy. All I knew was how to save, but I realized saving can only get you so far. I had very little knowledge when it came to navigating the world of finances. I had very little guidance or support. The first moment when I could manage my finances on my own, I thought I was doing great because I was good at making and saving money.

It wasn't until after graduating from the University of Washington and getting my first professional job as a Financial Services Professional that I realized… I was not at all great at managing my finances. I realized that during my entire college experience, I was losing hundreds and thousands of dollars because…

   ✕ I did NOT know how to better allocate my money.
   ✕ I was making all the WRONG investments.
   ✕ I wasn't willing to invest in myself.
   ✕ I believed money needed to be held onto.

Then I had a huge breakthrough, "I am not anywhere near where I want to be in my desired financial life." As heart-wrenching as that felt, it made me completely switch my mindset. That is when I knew:

- If I wanted real growth, I needed to get out of my comfort zone, stop making excuses, and take action.
- I needed to accept the support and guidance from the mentors and coaches who were already where I wanted to be.
- I needed to stop allowing my limiting money beliefs to interfere with my progress.

This realization helped me transform my entire journey. I finally accepted support from mentors and coaches. I opened myself up to the guidance I needed and created a clear action plan. I finally took action and learned every step of the way. Most importantly, I learned how to invest in a manner that would lead to great financial gains. This was the wake-up call I needed all along.

Fast forward to today —

I have several businesses that give me constant returns.

I have multiple streams of income.

I know how to grow my money through investing and minimizing risks.

I am teaching high-achieving female entrepreneurs and women of color to do the same!

When I look back, all I can say now is: "It's funny how bad investment decisions led me to understand the importance of investing with knowledge and strategy." And I am on a mission to make sure others don't make the same mistakes.

We all want to impact more people, and scale our business and revenue so we can spend quality time with our family doing what we love! To do this, we have to make sure we are managing, growing, and protecting our money properly. So, I want to share with you what has helped me do exactly that in my mompreneur journey!

TIP #1 Invest in Yourself First

Investing in yourself first is going to be key to your growth and the growth of your business. But what does it mean to invest in yourself first? Investing in yourself first means putting in the time, money, and energy towards the things that are going to help you grow in every aspect of your life—mentally, physically, spiritually, and emotionally. Instead of focusing on things that will not increase your wealth and wellness in the long term, look for ways to expand your knowledge on things that will get you to where you want to be in your life, business, and finances!

When you spend time, money, and energy on yourself, you are taking care of yourself first. You are telling the universe that you are ready to receive and opening the doors to abundance. When you allow yourself to give and receive you will notice you have a greater effect on others and the world!

TIP #2 Foster An Abundance Mindset

As a mompreneur, you have the power to create abundance in all areas of life. This is why you need to view the world through the lens of abundance. Viewing the world through abundance instead of scarcity will help you see others as potential collaborators, rather than competitors who are out to take from you.

To foster an abundance mindset:

1. Focus on what you have.
2. Surround yourself with people that think abundantly.
3. Create win-win situations.
4. Practice gratitude in your daily life.
5. Train your mind to look for solutions instead of problems.

Not only will you become more open to opportunities and new experiences, but you will attract authentic support systems into your life. This can show up in the form of a valuable network of friends, family, colleagues, and collaborators.

In fostering an abundance mindset, you will grow in health, wealth, and wellness!

#2 Become a Savvy Spender

To grow your business successfully you need to invest in the things that are going to give you great returns, and we can do this by taking educated risks. I'm talking again about investing in yourself, investing in the market, in real estate, and in ever-evolving investments like crypto!

Having a good strategy and a plan will help minimize risks.

#3 Know How To Delegate Your Money

A successful entrepreneur looks at each problem and considers how valuable their time is compared to the price to solve the problem. They know how much their time is worth and value getting things done more efficiently to spend their time on other tasks that will bring them greater returns.

An example of that is, "It takes me quite some time to get through all my emails, and this is taking from the time I could be taking client calls."

This could be a sign you need more support and can hire someone like a virtual assistant to help you get your time back!

#4 Diversify Your Revenue Streams

Economists can only theorize when market conditions will shift, and you'll be better able to thrive in a downturn if you have income from multiple sources. To diversify your existing revenues is to protect yourself and your business against life's unpredictable ups and downs. The COVID pandemic has shown us how easy it is for people to lose their jobs in unforeseen circumstances. Diversifying also allows growth!

Lastly, the main advice in all of these tips has been: start investing. To build wealth and live a life of freedom, you absolutely want to start investing. Start small and think of an amount you feel comfortable investing. Educate yourself on how different investment options work and how they're likely to behave.

Finally, remember this:

"To be a star you must shine your own light, follow your own path, and don't worry about the darkness, for that is when the stars shine brightest."
— Ralph Waldo Emerson

I hope this inspires you to believe in all your mom magic and to pursue everything you have ever dreamed of!

Melanie Greenhalgh

Founder of Collective Wisdom Coaching and Consulting

https://www.facebook.com/CollectiveWisdomCC
https://www.instagram.com/collectivewisdomcoaching
https://www.linkedin.com/in/melaniegreenhalgh/
https://collectivewisdomcoaching.com/

Melanie Greenhalgh is a mother, community worker, entrepreneur, public speaker, and author. She is not afraid to speak on the issues that are taboo, confronting, and uncomfortable. She speaks on issues of loss, grief, the growth that follows and how we can find our way back from surviving to thriving. Her speaking and media appearances include her signature TEDx talk – Let's Rethink our Approach to Grief and Loss.

Mel is a powerful storyteller as she shares her experiences with raw honesty that helps others understand that the losses we experience, and our reactions are part of the whole human experience.

When not absorbed in a gripping page-turner, Mel loves being with her friends (who are her family), eating, laughing, and otherwise spends far too much time at the computer. She lives on a property in Australia, with her husband and two remaining children (as two have flown the nest).

SHOWING UP IS WHAT MATTERS

By Melanie Greenhalgh

Perhaps it was her kind and gentle voice: "Melanie, time to wake up. How are you feeling honey?" Or perhaps it was the feeling of her soft hand gently touching my shoulder as I lay beneath several warm hospital blankets. I'll never really know, but her tenderness and caring at that moment allowed me to let go of all my fear, worry, trauma, and all the responsibility I had perched upon my shoulders for the last decade. It started with a single silent tear and then erupted into violent, ugly sobbing. It wouldn't stop.

As I finally managed to find my voice, I asked, "Is it gone?"

"Yes honey," she replied. "You're going to be okay."

It was Easter 2017, I was blearily waking from an intense six-hour operation. I'd undergone a radical hysterectomy, including the removal of my ovaries, after being diagnosed with endometrial cancer. It became the full stop on what I now call the 'Decade of Disaster.'

The 'Decade of Disaster' began with the diagnosis of my Mum's breast cancer at the tender young age of 49. What followed was five years of treatment and, eventually, palliative care. I whispered my goodbye on the morning of 5 January 2009, unsure of how I would navigate the world without my number one cheerleader by my side.

Six months later, I was woken by a phone call. Looking at the clock, I knew it wasn't good. Standing on the icy cold floorboards with warm sleep in my eyes, I listened to a voice tell me that my sister had suffered a pulmonary embolism and died as she walked towards the ambulance. She was 24.

I immediately went to her two children, Jackson aged five, and baby

Jesse aged 14 months. I was on autopilot, driven by my primal urge to protect my nephews from the violent man my sister was trapped in a relationship with. My mumma instincts knew exactly what to do. I sold him a story and calmly told him he would be in their future. I lied, knowing that I was there to extricate them on that winter's morning and knowing that my role was to keep them safe and to fight for them. As I drove those little boys toward their new home, their new siblings, and their new life I promised to love them, keep them safe, and be there for them for the rest of their lives. With that promise, I instantly went from being a mum of two to a mum of four beautiful children.

Time revealed to me that this was when I began living with a very complicated and deep sense of grief. The result was a confusing and guilt-ridden sense of motherhood. Sometimes I loved it, sometimes I hated it, and most of the time I felt an ever-present pressure for every decision to be perfect. I'd convinced myself that I was being judged by my Mum and sister from beyond.

Each child was carrying their own sense of loss and grief. To help them heal, I held them close. I was a lioness watching over her cubs, letting them safely play and experience the world, while trying to protect them from the threats that lay just beyond the horizon. I was, and always will be, willing to die for all of my children.

Living with such profound loss created a numbness in me. I silently buffered and swallowed my grief. I kept myself busy caring for others while I wilfully left myself neglected. I clearly understand now that I was experiencing survivor guilt and survivor anger—why did they leave me behind? Why did I have to mop up the mess? I experienced such deep distress and darkness that the only way to protect myself was to disconnect. I was present on the surface, but my mind was numbing my senses. I was living in fear and constantly anticipating the next wave of pain.

Then came a tsunami-sized wave of pain: we lost our family home. Our home burnt to the ground on a cold Winter's day. No one was hurt, but everything was gone. My childhood photos, the mementos of my sister's life, and all evidence of my Mum's existence turned to ash.

I went into overdrive to rebuild our life. I was a woman on a mission, and my motivation was to ensure those children were cocooned in love. When the house fell silent, I found the nights difficult. Severe insomnia whilst shrouded in darkness felt like the loneliest place on earth. I would ruminate and feel the suffering on a cellular level, internally raging whilst I tried to understand why this had happened to me. I bargained with myself. I analysed my behaviour. I reflected on what I had done to deserve it all. I didn't find the answers I was looking for. I was stuck in my grief.

Each morning the sun would rise, and one, two, maybe three, or even four little people would crawl into my bed vying for the prime position to be able to stroke my face and ask me gently what was for breakfast. That connection and sense of belonging was just enough. I used it as fuel to get up, sit on the edge of the bed, and make a deal with myself: to be there for those little people one moment at a time.

I eventually returned home from the hospital following my operation, and my oncologist told me he was pleased with the outcome. He laid out a recovery plan and told me that he clearly saw how much I loved my children, how hard I was fighting to keep them safe, and that if he had anything to do with it I would be there for them to see their lives unfold.

Maybe it was because the words came from a relative stranger, maybe it was because he was a man who had witnessed more than his fair share of loss and understood how the tidal waves of grief can consume us. I'll never really know, but his words were powerful. His intent was compassionate, and his words arrived with a strong message: keep showing up Mel.

And I did.

While recovering, I pitched my story to TEDx and was invited to take the stage. I worked for six months crafting my message. I immersed myself in learning all I could about the brain, the mind, the impact of trauma, and the power we possess to shift and recalibrate.

Releasing the cancer released so much more in me. I had a renewed sense of energy, and I used it to unpack and understand who I really was. I turned a lens on myself and did the work. It was painful, uncomfortable, tiring, and I often wanted to abandon myself and continue living on autopilot. But day in and day out I chose to love my children, fight to keep them safe and be there for them for the rest of my life.

Then it was time to deliver a very raw and personal story on a stage in front of my peers, my community, and my entire world. What I discovered that day was my true purpose: storytelling. Connecting with people and sharing my message—that we are never alone and that asking for help is a strength. The reaction to my sharing my experiences was powerful and set me on a process of discovery about how I could bring more hope into the world.

Discovering my how, my purpose, my message, and my contribution hasn't been easy. There have been false starts, mistakes, and lots of learning. Five years on, I am a 46-year-old woman, a mother of four young people, and a wife to one beautiful and supportive man. I am also the founder and CEO of Collective Wisdom Coaching and Consulting, and I am writing the next chapter of my life. I am exactly where I need to be right now. I have good and bad days. I have positive and negative conversations with myself. I see light and shade in life. I am shifting away from pursuing perfection. I am grateful for the pain and loss I experienced because it allowed me to find my way to a more caring, compassionate, and calm relationship with myself.

My wisdom is wider and deeper for living through the 'Decade of Disaster.' It is powerful, all-encompassing, and transformative. I have all the evidence I'll ever need to prove that I'm a survivor. I understand what it means to have the whole human experience.

I learned that showing up is all that matters.

JOIN THE MOVEMENT!
#I&PM

Inspired & Profitable Mompreneurs
With The Inspired & Profitable Mompreneur

The Inspired & Profitable Mompreneur was created by Angela Bell, to serve the need she saw and experienced as a mom; the need for time & financial freedom and flexibility. She is the podcast hosts of the *Inspired & Profitable Mompreneur Podcast*, Amazon best-selling author and motivational speaker who travels the world. Angela is the movement creator of #I&PM – Inspired & Profitable Mompreneurs: The movement has been created to empower moms around the world to live their best life, create time & financial freedom via their own business, and use their power to create a better world! The Inspired & Profitable Mompreneur educates, celebrates, and empowers Moms globally.

THE
INSPIRED & PROFITABLE
MOMPRENEUR
A community of Moms improving their
lives, their communities and the world!

Looking to Join Us in our Next Anthology or Publish YOUR Own?

The Inspired & Profitable Mompreneur offers full-service publishing, marketing, book tour, and campaign services. For more information, contact info@angelabell.ca

We are always looking for women who want to share their stories and expertise and feature their businesses on our podcasts, in our books, and in our magazines.

www.ingramcontent.com/pod-product-compliance
Lightning Source LLC
Chambersburg PA
CBHW060331130626
46553CB00003B/968